Randall Thomas Davidson

Origin and History of the Lambeth Conferences of 1867 and 1878

With the official reports and resolutions

Randall Thomas Davidson

Origin and History of the Lambeth Conferences of 1867 and 1878
With the official reports and resolutions

ISBN/EAN: 9783744747639

Printed in Europe, USA, Canada, Australia, Japan

Cover: Foto ©ninafisch / pixelio.de

More available books at **www.hansebooks.com**

Origin and History

OF

The Lambeth Conferences

OF

1867 AND 1878,

With the Official Reports and Resolutions.

EDITED BY

RANDALL T. DAVIDSON,

DEAN OF WINDSOR.

LONDON:
SOCIETY FOR PROMOTING CHRISTIAN KNOWLEDGE,
NORTHUMBERLAND AVENUE, CHARING CROSS, W.C.;
43, QUEEN VICTORIA STREET, E.C.
BRIGHTON: 135, NORTH STREET.

NEW YORK: E. & J. B. YOUNG & Co.
1888.

CONTENTS.

PART I.

NARRATIVE.

CHAP. I.—The First Conference, 1867 ... ... *page* 5
CHAP. II.—The Second Conference, 1878 16

PART II.

DOCUMENTS, REPORTS, AND RESOLUTIONS, ILLUSTRATING THE HISTORY OF THE CONFERENCES OF 1867 AND 1878.

I.—Letters from the Canadian Bishops: Reply of the Archbishop of Canterbury ... *page* 32
II.—Action taken by the Convocation of Canterbury 36
III.—Official "Programme of Arrangements" issued by the Archbishop of Canterbury for the Conference of 1867 37
IV.—Archbishop Longley's Opening Address, Sept. 24, 1867 42
V.—Amended Programme adopted during the Sessions 48
VI.—Formal "Address to the Faithful" from the Bishops attending the Conference of 1867 ... 53
VII.—Latin and Greek Versions of the Address ... 57
VIII.—Resolutions formally passed by the Conference of 1867 62

IX.—Correspondence with Dean Stanley about the use of Westminster Abbey ... ... *page* 66

X.—Reports of the Committees appointed by the Conference of 1867 72

XI.—Resolutions of the Conference adopted at the Adjourned Session, Dec. 10, 1867 98

XII.—Addresses from the Canadian and West Indian Houses of Bishops, 1872 and 1873 101

XIII.—Correspondence between the Bishops of the Protestant Episcopal Church in the United States and the Archbishop of Canterbury, 1874 and 1875 103

XIV.—Memorandum of the Canadian House of Bishops, 1874 110

XV.—Action of the Convocations of Canterbury and York with reference to the proposed Second Conference 111

XVI.—Circular Letter of Inquiry addressed by the Archbishop of Canterbury to all the Anglican Bishops. March 28, 1876 113

XVII.—Letter of invitation to the Conference of 1878, dated July 10, 1877 115

XVIII.—Formal "Letter" of the Bishops attending the Conference of 1878 117

XIX.—Latin and Greek Versions of the Letter ... 145

XX.—Official List of the Bishops present at the Conference of 1878 158

XXI.—Order of precedence observed at the Conference of 1878 159

XXII.—Invitations issued for the Conference of 1888 ... 161

NARRATIVE.

CHAPTER I.

THE FIRST CONFERENCE. 1867.

PERHAPS it is not too much to say that a decennial Conference of the bishops of the Anglican Communion, under the presidency of the Archbishop of Canterbury, has now become a recognised part of the organisation of our Church, and it may be interesting to many, at the moment when the third of these Conferences is about to assemble at Lambeth, to recall the history and doings of the earlier gatherings of 1867 and 1878.

The first official step in connexion with the assembling of such a Conference was taken, not in England, but in Canada. The notion had, indeed, been "in the air" for many years,[1] both in England and abroad, and the final impulse which brought about a Conference was eminently significant of the changed conditions of the Church.

It arose, strange to say, from the interest awakened in North America by the Church affairs of South Africa.

At the Provincial Synod of the Canadian Church, held on September 20, 1865, it was unanimously agreed, upon the motion of the Bishop of Ontario, to urge upon the Archbishop of Canterbury and the Convocation of his Province that means should be

---

[1] A reference to some of the earlier suggestions on the subject will be found in the *Guardian* of June 19, 1878, p. 857.

adopted "by which the members of our Anglican Communion in all quarters of the world should have a share in the deliberations for her welfare, and be permitted to have a representation in one General Council of her members gathered from every land."[1]

To a more personal appeal which accompanied this address, Archbishop Longley replied in guarded terms. "The meeting of such a Synod," he said, "is not by any means foreign to my own feelings.... I cannot, however, take any step in so grave a matter without consulting my episcopal brethren in both branches of the united Church of England and Ireland, as well as those in the different colonies and dependencies of the British Empire."

In May, 1866, the Convocation of Canterbury appointed a committee to "consider and report upon" the Canadian address, and the whole subject was fully debated in Convocation in the following spring. Obvious difficulties and dangers were suggested, but in the end the Lower House conveyed to the Archbishop of Canterbury "a respectful expression of an earnest desire that he would be pleased to issue an invitation to all the bishops in communion with the Church of England, to assemble at such time and place, and accompanied by such persons as may be deemed fit, for the purpose of Christian sympathy and mutual counsel on matters affecting the welfare of the Church at home and abroad."[2]

In the Upper House, Archbishop Longley took the utmost pains to "diminish the doubts and difficulties" of some of his brethren. "It should be distinctly understood," he said, "that at this meeting no declaration of faith shall be made, and no decision come to what shall affect generally the interests of

---

[1] For the full text of the address and reply, see Part II., No. I., p. 32, and Chronicle of Convocation of Canterbury, May 2, 1866, p. 286; Feb. 12, 1867, p. 696.

[2] Chronicle of Convocation, Feb. 14, 1867, p. 793.

the Church, but that we shall meet together for brotherly counsel and encouragement . . . . I should refuse to convene any assembly which pretended to enact any canons, or affected to make any decisions binding on the Church . . . . I feel I undertake a great responsibility in assenting to this request, and certainly if I saw anything approaching to what [is apprehended] as likely to result from it, I should not be disposed to sanction it, but I can assure [my brethren] that I should enter on this meeting in the full confidence that nothing would pass but that which tended to brotherly love and union, and would bind the Colonial Church, which is certainly in a most unsatisfactory state, more closely to the Mother Church." [1]

A week later the Archbishop issued the following invitation to all the bishops of the Anglican Communion, then 144 in number:—

"LAMBETH PALACE, *Feb.* 22, 1867.

RIGHT REV. AND DEAR BROTHER,—

"I request your presence at a meeting of the bishops in visible communion with the United Church of England and Ireland, purposed (God willing) to be holden at Lambeth, under my presidency, on the 24th of September next and the three following days.

"The circumstances under which I have resolved to issue the present invitation are these:—The Metropolitan and Bishops of Canada, last year, addressed to the two Houses of the Convocation of Canterbury the expression of their desire that I should be moved to invite the bishops of our Indian and Colonial Episcopate to meet myself and the Home bishops for brotherly communion and conference.

"The consequence of that appeal has been that

---

[1] Chronicle of Convocation, Feb. 15, 1867, p. 807.

both Houses of the Convocation of my province have addressed to me their dutiful request that I would invite the attendance, not only of our Home and Colonial bishops, but of all who are avowedly in communion with our Church. The same request was unanimously preferred to me at a numerous gathering of English, Irish, and Colonial archbishops and bishops recently assembled at Lambeth; at which,—I rejoice to record it,—we had the counsel and concurrence of an eminent bishop of the Church in the United States of America,—the Bishop of Illinois.

"Moved by these requests, and by the expressed concurrence therein of other members both of the Home and Colonial episcopate, who could not be present at our meeting, I have now resolved,—not, I humbly trust, without the guidance of God the Holy Ghost,—to grant this grave request, and call together the meeting thus earnestly desired. I greatly hope that you may be able to attend it, and to aid us with your presence and brotherly counsel thereat.

"I propose that, at our assembling, we should first solemnly seek the blessing of Almighty God on our gathering, by uniting together in the highest act of the Church's worship. After this, brotherly consultations will follow. In these we may consider together many practical questions, the settlement of which would tend to the advancement of the kingdom of our Lord and Master Jesus Christ, and to the maintenance of greater union in our missionary work, and to increased intercommunion among ourselves.

"Such a meeting would not be competent to make declarations or lay down definitions on points of doctrine. But united worship and common counsels would greatly tend to maintain practically the unity of the faith; whilst they would bind us in straiter bonds of peace and brotherly charity.

"I shall gladly receive from you a list of any subjects you may wish to suggest to me for consideration and discussion. Should you be unable to attend, and desire to commission any brother bishop to speak for you, I shall welcome him as your representative in our united deliberations.

"But I must once more express my earnest hope that, on this solemn occasion, I may have the great advantage of your personal presence.

"And now I commend this proposed meeting to your fervent prayers; and, humbly beseeching the blessing of Almighty God on yourself and your diocese, I subscribe myself,

"Your faithful brother in the Lord,
"C. T. CANTUAR."

The invitation was accepted by seventy-six bishops, and as soon as those who came from the Colonies and the United States began to arrive in England, a series of preliminary meetings was held to discuss and arrange the details of a Conference for which no precedent existed to serve as a guide. The strong divergence of opinion upon the legal aspect of Bishop Colenso's deposition and excommunication, and the fact that the Bishop of Capetown had come to England on purpose to secure, if possible, the synodical sanction of the Conference to the course he had himself adopted, made the agenda-paper a matter of no small difficulty, if it was to be kept within the limits laid down by the Archbishop of Canterbury in the Convocation speech which has been quoted above. Not a few of the English bishops felt so sure of the increased confusion such a Conference must cause in an already tangled web that they declined to attend its deliberations. Among these were the Archbishop of York and the Bishops of Durham, Carlisle, Ripon, Peterborough, and Manchester. Others, including Bishop Thirlwall, of St. David's, postponed their acceptance until the official agenda-paper or programme should be published,[1] a fact to which they afterwards called attention when the programme had unexpectedly been changed.

The Conference met on Tuesday, September 24,

---

[1] For its full text, see Part II., No. III., p. 37.

the opening service being preceded by a Celebration of Holy Communion in Lambeth Palace Chapel, with a sermon from Bishop Whitehouse, of Illinois. The meetings of the Conference were held in the upstairs dining-hall, or "guard-room," of Lambeth Palace, not (as was the case in 1878) in the great library. On the Archbishop of Canterbury's right sat the Archbishop of Armagh, the Bishop of London, the Presiding Bishop of the American Church, the Primus of the Scottish Episcopal Church, the Bishop of Calcutta, and the Bishop of Sydney. On the left were the Archbishop of Dublin, and the Bishops of Montreal, New Zealand, and Capetown. The other bishops sat in front. The Bishop of Gloucester and Bristol acted as episcopal secretary to the meeting throughout its deliberations.

In his opening address,[1] Archbishop Longley again defined, with some care, the position of the Conference. "It has never been contemplated," he said, "that we should assume the functions of a general synod of all the churches in full communion with the Church of England, and take upon ourselves to enact canons that should be binding upon those here represented. We merely propose to discuss matters of practical interest, and pronounce what we deem expedient in resolutions which may serve as safe guides to future action. Thus it will be seen that our first essay is rather tentative and experimental, in a matter in which we have no distinct precedent to direct us."

Special importance attached to the discussions of the first day, when, in the form of a preamble to the subsequent resolutions, the standpoint taken by the Anglican Church was in general terms described. All the leading bishops took part in the debate, and its outcome will be best seen by placing the paragraph, as it was first drafted, side by side with the form which was finally agreed upon.

---

[1] See Part II., No. IV., p. 42.

As originally drafted.	*As ultimately carried.*
"We, Bishops of Christ's Holy Catholic Church, professing the faith of the primitive and undivided Church, as based on Scripture, defined by the first four General Councils,[1] and reaffirmed by the Fathers of the English Reformation, now assembled by the good providence of God at the Archiepiscopal Palace of Lambeth, under the presidency of the Primate of all England, desire, first, to give hearty thanks to Almighty God for having thus brought us together for common counsels and united worship; secondly, we desire to express the deep sorrow with which we view the divided condition of the flock of Christ throughout the world; and, lastly, we do here solemnly declare our belief that the best hope of future reunion will be found in drawing each of us for ourselves closer to our common Lord, in giving ourselves to much prayer and intercession, in the cultivation of a spirit of charity, and in seeking to diffuse through every part of the Christian community that desire and resolution to return to the faith and discipline of the undivided Church which was the principle of the English Reformation."	"We, Bishops of Christ's Holy Catholic Church, in visible Communion with the United Church of England and Ireland, professing the faith delivered to us in Holy Scripture, maintained by the primitive Church and by the Fathers of the English Reformation, now assembled by the good providence of God, at the Archiepiscopal Palace of Lambeth, under the presidency of the Primate of all England, desire, first, to give hearty thanks to Almighty God for having thus brought us together for common counsels and united worship; secondly, we desire to express the deep sorrow with which we view the divided condition of the flock of Christ throughout the world, ardently longing for the fulfilment of the prayer of our Lord: 'That all may be one, as Thou, Father, art in me, and I in Thee, that they also may be one in us, that the world may believe that Thou has sent me'; and, lastly, we do here solemnly record our conviction that unity will be most effectually promoted, by maintaining the faith in its purity and integrity, as taught in the Holy Scriptures, held by the primitive Church, summed up in the Creeds, and affirmed by the undisputed General Councils, and by drawing each of us closer to our common Lord, by giving ourselves to much prayer and intercession, by the cultivation of a spirit of charity, and a love of the Lord's appearing."

---

[1] *See* 1 Eliz. ch. i. xxxvi.

On the second day—Wednesday, September 25—the president consented, notwithstanding the strenuous protest of several bishops, to a complete change of programme, in accordance with the wish of the Bishop of Capetown and others,[1] and the discussions were thus diverted into an unexpected channel. A long day was occupied in discussing the due gradation of synodal authority, diocesan, provincial, and, perhaps, patriarchal, within the Anglican Communion. After the failure of successive attempts to obtain the formal sanction of the Conference to the definite schemes proposed, it was found necessary to fall back upon a perfectly general resolution proposed by Bishop Selwyn, of New Zealand, in the following terms :—" That, in the opinion of this Conference, unity of faith and discipline will be best maintained among the several branches of the Anglican Communion by due and canonical subordination of the synods of the several branches to the higher authority of a synod or synods above them."

This was carried *nem. con.*, and a committee was appointed to consider the whole subject.

On the following day (Thursday, Sept. 26), the " burning question " of Bishop Colenso's position was the subject of prolonged debate. The Archbishop of Canterbury had declined to allow any distinct resolution of condemnation to be put to the Conference, and he ruled out of order a motion to that effect which was proposed by the Presiding Bishop of the American Church. After several hours discussion, it was resolved, by 49 votes to 10, " that, in the judgment of the bishops here assembled, the whole Anglican Communion is deeply injured by the present condition of the Church in Natal ; and that a committee be now appointed at this general meeting to report on the best mode by which the

---

[1] See Part II., No. V., p. 48.

Church may be delivered from the continuance of this scandal, and the truth maintained. That such report be forwarded to his Grace the Lord Archbishop of Canterbury with the request that his Grace will be pleased to transmit the same to all the bishops of the Anglican Communion, and to ask for their judgment thereon."

The next matter dealt with was the possible constitution of what was described as a Spiritual Court of Appeal; and on this subject it was found necessary, after long debate, to await the report of a committee before any formal recommendation could be made. Such a committee was accordingly appointed " to consider the constitution of a voluntary spiritual tribunal, to which questions of doctrine may be carried by appeal from the tribunals for the exercise of discipline in each Province of the Colonial Church."

It had, upon the previous day, been informally decided that a short "Encyclical" Letter or Address should be drafted by a Committee[1] for the signature of the Bishops attending the Conference. This Address was adopted by the whole body before the adjournment on Thursday evening, and was formally signed at the morning session on the following day.[2] It was suggested in the Conference that it should be publicly read by the Archbishop from the altar of Lambeth Parish Church; but this course was not adopted. After other resolutions[3] had been carried with respect to the due notification of the establishment of new dioceses, the provision of Letters Commendatory, and the proper measure of publicity to

---

[1] The Committee consisted of the Archbishop of Canterbury and the Bishops of London, Winchester, Oxford, North Carolina, Grahamstown, Ohio, Ely, St. Andrews, Cape Town, Moray and Ross, and New Zealand.

[2] The complete document, as signed, is given below. Part II., No. VI., p. 53.

[3] See Part II., No. VIII., p. 62.

be given to the proceedings of the Conference, a second and unexpected debate arose upon the position of Bishop Colenso, and a resolution was carried expressing the acquiescence of the Conference in certain advice given by the Convocation of Canterbury a year before, respecting the steps to be taken " if it be decided that a New Bishop should be consecrated " for the Diocese of Natal.

After the *Gloria in Excelsis* had been sung by the assembled Bishops, the Primate dismissed the Conference with the Benediction, on the understanding that those members of it who could remain in England should reassemble in December to receive the Reports of the various Committees.

On the following day, Saturday, September 28, thirty-four Bishops attended a closing service in Lambeth Parish Church, when the Holy Communion was celebrated by the Archbishop, and a sermon was preached by Bishop Fulford, of Montreal. It had originally been proposed that this service should be held in Westminster Abbey; but Dean Stanley, in a correspondence published at the time,[1] gave his reasons for objecting to the use of the Abbey in the manner proposed, and the Conference fell back on Lambeth Church as an alternative.

The several Committees were in frequent session during the next two months under the direction of Bishop Selwyn, of New Zealand;[2] Bishop Fulford, of Montreal; and Bishop Cotterill, of Grahamstown, the last-named of whom had undertaken the onerous work of " Secretary of Committees " to the Conference.

On December 10 a further session of the Conference, or such members of it as had remained in

---

[1] See Part II., No. IX., p. 66.
[2] Bishop Selwyn had been nominated in November, 1867, to the See of Lichfield; but he was not enthroned till January 9, 1868.

England, was held at Lambeth Palace, when eight Reports were presented.[1] With reference to the first seven of these, a resolution was in each case formally passed: "That this adjourned meeting of the Conference receives the Report (No. —) of the Committee now presented, and directs the publication thereof, commending it to the careful consideration of the Bishops of the Anglican Communion, as containing the result of the deliberations of that Committee; and returns the members of the same its thanks for the care with which they have considered the various important questions referred to them."

Upon the presentation of Report No. VIII., which referred to Bishop Colenso's deposition, it was resolved "that the Report be received and printed; that the thanks of this meeting be given to the Committee for their labours, and that his Grace be requested to communicate the Report to the Council of the Colonial Bishoprics Fund."

The further resolutions, which will be found in full elsewhere,[2] were for the most part of a formal character. It was, indeed, impossible, considering the small number of Bishops who were able to attend, that any important motions should at this stage be brought before them. The session lasted for a few hours only, and it became evident that in any future Conference some different arrangement must be adopted. Reiterated thanks were expressed to the Bishops of Gloucester and Grahamstown, the Episcopal Secretaries; and to Mr. Philip Wright and Mr. Isambard Brunel, who had acted as their lay assistants and advisers. The Conference had been attended, in all, by seventy-six Bishops out of one hundred and forty-four who had received invitations. Of these seventy-six, eighteen were English Bishops,

---

[1] See Part II., No. X., p. 72.
[2] See Part II., No. XI., p. 98.

five were Irish, and six were Scotch. The Colonial Church sent twenty-four, including five Metropolitans. The United States sent nineteen. At no one session of the Conference were all the Bishops present, but the Encyclical Address received the signatures of all, and the President was subsequently authorised to affix the names of several others who had been reluctantly prevented from attending.[1]

CHAPTER II.

THE SECOND CONFERENCE. 1878.

THE circumstances in which the first Conference had been held were exceptionally difficult, and some of the interests at stake were of so keen and even personal a sort that the Bishops found it hard to give undistracted attention to the wider questions of policy and practice which had been included in Archbishop Longley's programme. The allotted time also had been far too short for dealing adequately with such subjects. Eight Committees had indeed reported; but their Reports, as has been seen, were presented to less than a score of Bishops at one brief session on a single day. Due discussion of them was thus impossible, and Bishop Selwyn, who had been foremost perhaps among the promoters

---

[1] See Part II., No. XI., p. 98.

A Second Conference Asked for.

of the gathering, could only suggest the postponement to a future Conference of any debate upon these weighty documents.[1]

The inquiry soon became common, Will there be a second Conference, and if so, when? Once again, as in 1865, it was the Canadian Church which took the first official step. In December, 1872, the Bishops of the Ecclesiastical Province of Canada made formal appeal to the Convocation of Canterbury to join with them in a request to Archbishop Tait, who had in 1869 succeeded to the Primacy, that he would summon as soon as possible a second meeting of the Conference.[2]

Taking this Canadian letter as his text, Bishop Selwyn, in a memorable speech in Convocation, endorsed and expanded the appeal. He had visited America in 1871. He was to pay a second and more formal visit in 1874, and his experience in every part of the world led him to long for such confederation and unity of action as could, he believed, be best secured by a second Conference, or, as he called it, "A General Council of the Bishops of the Anglican Communion, to carry on the work begun by the Lambeth Conference of 1867."[3]

The matter was, by common consent, adjourned for a time; and in the following year (1874) Bishop Kerfoot, of Pittsburgh, as representing the American Church, was in constant communication upon the subject with Archbishop Tait, whom he visited at Addington, and to whom he was authorised to write officially from America.[4] The Bishop of Lichfield's formal attendance in that year at the meetings, first

---

[1] See e.g., "Chronicle of Convocation," Feb. 13, 1873, p. 172.
[2] See Part II., No. XII., p. 101.
[3] See "Chronicle of Convocation," Feb. 13, 1873, pp. 168–174.
[4] See Part II., No. XIII., p. 103, and "Life of Bishop Kerfoot," vol. ii., pp. 581–587.

of the Provincial Synod of Canada and then of the General Convention in New York,[1] brought the question again into prominence, and it had now become practically certain that a second Conference would be held in 1877 or 1878 if the necessary conditions could be agreed upon.

Some of these conditions were suggested by the Canadian House of Bishops;[2] others were laid down by the Archbishop himself in an important Convocation speech, and in his written reply to a formal request signed by no less than 43 Bishops of the American Church.[3] Speaking in Convocation on April 16, 1875, he said:—

"No one can doubt that very great good has arisen from the friendly intercourse which took place during the last Lambeth Conference. At the same time, it must be remembered that it is a serious matter to gather the Bishops together from all parts of the globe, unless there is some distinct object for their so gathering. I therefore am disposed, by the advice of my brethren, to request that our brethren at home, and also those at a distance, will state to me as explicitly as possible what the subjects are that it is desirable to discuss at such meeting. They are of a somewhat limited character. There is no intention whatever on the part of anybody to gather together the Bishops of the Anglican Church for the sake of defining any matter of doctrine. Our doctrines are contained in our formularies, and our formularies are interpreted by the proper judicial authorities, and there is no intention whatever at any such gathering that questions of doctrine should be submitted for interpretation in any future Lambeth Conference any more than they were at the previous Lambeth Conference. My predecessor had a very

---

[1] See "Life of Bishop Selwyn," vol. ii., pp. 319–324.
[2] See Part II., No. XIV., p. 110.
[3] See Part II., No. XIII, p. 103.

difficult task in defining the exact duty of the Bishops who came together on the former occasion, and with great firmness, and at the same time with that remarkable courtesy and kindliness for which he was so eminent, he steered the somewhat difficult course which was before him, and it was distinctly settled that matters of that kind were not to be entered upon. Well, then, with regard to discipline, of course our discipline is exercised by ourselves and by the constituted Courts of the Church at home, and the discipline of the various Colonial and more independent Churches is exercised by these Churches according to fixed rules which have been established by themselves, and we have no intention whatever of interfering with these matters of discipline. We are, therefore, perhaps naturally, anxious to know tolerably distinctly the subjects which any would wish to bring before us. . . . . Friendly intercourse must, of course, be of great value. But it is possible that Bishops at a very great distance—such as the Bishop of Athabasca, who, I believe, can scarcely reach his diocese under a year—might perhaps, under a misapprehension, think it was necessarily their duty to come to such a Conference unless it was distinctly stated what was to be done. . . . . I cannot doubt that there are many points respecting the connection between the Mother Church and the Colonial Churches on which a friendly Conference would be very valuable indeed. . . . . With regard to our brethren in America, no such difficulties exist: what we enjoyed so much during the late Conference was the friendly intercourse and exchange of sentiment between us and them. We have no desire to interfere with their affairs, and I am sure they have no desire to interfere with ours. As far as they are concerned, I think it would be a work of love in which we should be engaged—the extension of Christ's kingdom—and that we may be able by friendly intercourse to strengthen each other's hands.

But I think it important that there should be no misunderstanding, and none of that difficulty which, I am bound to say, did exist at the last Lambeth Conference as to what subjects might and what subjects might not be introduced ; that we should know what it is that our brethren wish to bring before us, and what we wish to bring before them, before they give themselves the trouble of coming from the ends of the earth, happy as the results of such a meeting are, under God's Providence, likely to be." [1]

Fortified by the concurrence of the Northern Convocation,[2] which had held aloof in 1867, the Archbishop of Canterbury issued a formal letter on March 28th, 1876, to all the Bishops of the Anglican Communion, intimating his readiness to hold a Conference in 1878, " if it shall seem expedient, after the opinions of all our brethren have been ascertained," and inviting an expression of opinion.[3] These letters to the Bishops throughout the world were not, as heretofore, sent direct from Lambeth ; but were forwarded to the various Metropolitans and presiding Bishops, with a request that they would transmit them officially to the Bishops entitled to receive them in each branch or Province of the Church—a rule which has since been followed in all similar circulars of an official kind.

Before the close of the year about ninety letters of reply were received by the Archbishop, from all parts of the world, showing, as had been anticipated, an overwhelming preponderance of opinion in favour of a second Conference, provided a longer period of session could be arranged for than "the four short days" of 1867.

---

[1] See "Chronicle of Convocation," April 16, 1875, pp. 132–134.
[2] For the formal resolution passed in the Convocation of York on Feb. 26, 1875, see Part II., No. XV., p. 111.
[3] See Part II., No. XVI., p. 113.

Most of the Bishops also suggested subjects for discussion, and on these the Archbishop took counsel with an Episcopal Committee, and especially with Bishop Selwyn. After the fullest deliberation, the following definite invitation was issued :—

LAMBETH PALACE,
July 10, 1877.

RIGHT REVEREND AND DEAR BROTHER,

It is proposed to hold a Conference of Bishops of the Anglican Communion, at this place, beginning on Tuesday, the second day of July, eighteen hundred and seventy-eight.

The Conference, it is proposed, shall extend over four weeks; the first week, of Four Sessions, to be devoted to discussions, in Conference, of the subjects submitted for deliberation; the second and third weeks to the consideration of these subjects in Committees; and the fourth week to final discussions in Conference, and to the close of the meeting.

The subjects selected for discussion are the following :—

1. The best mode of maintaining Union among the various churches of the Anglican Communion.

2. Voluntary Boards of Arbitration for Churches to which such an arrangement may be applicable.

3. The relations to each other of Missionary Bishops and of Missionaries, in various branches of the Anglican Communion acting in the same country.

4. The position of Anglican Chaplains and Chaplaincies on the Continent of Europe and elsewhere.

5. Modern forms of infidelity, and the best means of dealing with them.

6. The condition, progress, and needs of the various Churches of the Anglican Communion.

I shall feel greatly obliged if, at your early convenience, you will inform me whether we may have the pleasure of expecting your presence at the Conference.

I am,
Right Reverend and dear Brother,
Yours faithfully in Christ,
A. C. CANTUAR.

It was evidently not without intention that the subjects selected for discussion, though grouped under such all-embracing headings, coincided in some parts so closely with the Resolutions of the Conference of 1867. The Reports presented in that year had never, as has been seen, received adequate discussion, nor had any one of them been "adopted" by the Conference. By a recurrence to these subjects a certain measure of continuity was secured, and a basis was laid for the practical deliberations of 1878. The plan adopted in 1867 of drafting and publishing beforehand the Resolutions which were to be moved, had not worked altogether well, and it was arranged that in 1878 the formal motion should in each case be for the appointment of a Committee which, after considering some branch of the selected subjects, should report to the Conference in its final week of session.

One hundred and eight Bishops accepted the Archbishop's invitation. Some of these, however, were at the last moment prevented from attending, and the actual number present at the Conference was exactly one hundred.

On Saturday, June 29, St. Peter's Day, the proceedings of the Conference began with a gathering of Bishops at Canterbury, for what had been described as a "Service of Welcome" in the Cathedral.

Archbishop Tait, four weeks before, had lost his only son, who had recently returned from a visit to America, and the fear that the Archbishop would himself be unable to attend the Service, which would thus be deprived of much of its interest and completeness, kept away many Bishops who had intended to be present. The Archbishop, however, went to Canterbury as arranged, and was met by thirty-six Bishops,[1] and an immense gathering of clergy.

A service was held in the morning in St. Augustine's Missionary College, with a sermon by Bishop Cleveland Coxe, of Western New York, and at the Special Evensong in the Cathedral at three o'clock, the Archbishop gave an official welcome to the assembled Bishops. The ancient marble throne, known as "St. Augustine's Chair," was moved from its ordinary position in the south transept, and placed in the centre of the altar steps. The Bishops were grouped on either side of it, and the Archbishop addressed them as follows :—

" My brothers, representatives of the Church throughout the world, engaged in spreading the Gospel of Jesus Christ wherever the sun shines, I esteem it a very high privilege to welcome you here to-day, to the cradle of Anglo-Saxon Christianity. . . I am addressing you from St. Augustine's chair. This thought carries us back to the time when that first missionary to our Anglo-Saxon forefathers, amid much discouragement, landed on these barbarous shores. More than twelve centuries and a-half have rolled on since then. The seed he sowed has borne an abundant harvest, and this great British nation, and our sister beyond the ocean, have cause to render thanks to God for the work begun by him here. And how full of encouragement to you is St. Augustine's work. What difficulties greater than those that confronted him can stand in your path? And you have blessings that he had not. You stand nearer the pure primitive Christianity of the Apostles. You have a motive power to touch the heart denied to him. . . . . The varied history of the Church has

---

[1] Nearly all of these came from abroad. Only three of the home Diocesans were present.

recorded many failures and many successes, and we learn from the past neither to be elated by the one nor discouraged by the other. The monuments which surround us speak of a chequered history. They tell of dark times and of great times. But they all testify to the superintending power of God, Who works all things according to the pleasure of His will, after His own plan for the building up of His one Kingdom in His own way. . . . .
It is my privilege to welcome you to Christ Church, Canterbury. . . . . Gregory sent St. Augustine here that he might mark England with the name of Christ, "that Name which is above every name." God grant that that Name may be ever more and more acknowledged among us; that its glories may shine more and more brightly here, and in your distant dioceses, triumphing over all obstacles, and reconciling all petty divisions, uniting all hearts in the truth of our Lord and Saviour, Jesus Christ. My Brethren from across the Atlantic,—you especially from the great Republic,—to you a particular welcome is due from me. Partly for our Church's sake, partly for my sake, partly also for something you discerned in himself, you welcomed one very dear to me last autumn.[1] The bond that unites us is not the less sacred because so many hopes of earthly joy have withered and disappeared. God unite us all more closely in His own great Family. And now let us to prayer."

At eleven o'clock, on Tuesday, July 2, the Bishops met at Lambeth. They were marshalled in the Guard-room, where the actual Sessions of 1867 had been held, and passed thence in procession to the Chapel, the Bishops from the United States walking alongside of the English Diocesan Bishops as their guests, all due precedence being given in the proces-

---

[1] The Archbishop's son, the Rev. Craufurd Tait, had been formally welcomed by the House of Bishops assembled at Boston on Oct. 5, 1877.

sional arrangements to the Metropolitans and presiding Bishops.[1] After the *Veni Creator* had been sung, the Holy Communion was celebrated by the Archbishop of Canterbury, assisted by the Bishops of London, Winchester, Salisbury, and Rochester, as officers of the Provincial College. With the exception of the Archbishop of Canterbury's Chaplains,[2] none but Bishops were present in the Chapel. The sermon was preached by the Archbishop of York, the text being Galatians ii. 2 : "But when Peter was come to Antioch, I withstood him to the face, because he was to be blamed."[3]

The Sessions of the Conference were held in the Great Library, not, as in 1867, in the Guard-room. The arrangement of hours and subjects was as follows :—

Tuesday, July 2.
- 11 a.m. Holy Communion and sermon in Lambeth Palace Chapel.
- 1.30 p.m. Archbishop's opening address.
- 2 p.m.—4.45 p.m. *Subject I.*— The best mode of maintaining union among the various Churches of the Anglican Communion.

Wednesday, July 3.
- 10.30 a.m. Litany in Chapel.
- 11 a.m. *Subject II.*—Voluntary Boards of Arbitration for Churches to which such an arrangement may be applicable.
- 1.30 p.m. *Subject III.*—The relation to each other of Missionary Bishops and of Missionaries in various Branches of the Anglican Communion, acting in the same country.

---

[1] See Part II., No. XXI., p. 159.

[2] Archdeacon Fisher, Rev. F. G. Blomfield, Hon. and Rev. W. H. Fremantle, Rev. W. F. Erskine Knollys, Rev. Randall T. Davidson.

[3] The sermon was published by Murray, under the title of "St. Peter at Antioch."

Thursday, July 4.
- 10.30 a.m.   Litany in Chapel.
- 11 a.m.   *Subject IV.*—The position of Anglican Chaplains and Chaplaincies on the Continent of Europe and elsewhere.
- 1.30 p.m.   *Subject V.*—Modern forms of Infidelity, and the best means of dealing with them.

Friday, July 5.
- 10.30 a.m.   Litany in Chapel.
- 11 a.m. and 1.30 p.m.   *Subject VI.*—The condition, progress, and needs of the various Churches of the Anglican Communion.

It was decided, almost unanimously, that the proceedings of the Conference should, as in 1867, be private. A short-hand report was made of all the speeches, and it was arranged that this should be preserved by the Archbishop along with the other manuscripts belonging to Lambeth Library, but should in no way be made public.[1]

The secretarial work of the Conference was again, as in 1867, under the charge of Bishops Ellicott and Cotterill,[2] assisted by Dr. Isambard Brunel, and, unofficially, by the Archbishop's resident Chaplain.[3] For the avoidance of discussions irrelevant to the programme it was arranged, with general consent, that if any memorials or petitions—and there were not a few—should be forwarded to the Conference, they should be placed, without further remark than a bare statement of their purport, in the hands of the

---

[1] A long account of the debates which had taken place in 1867 was unexpectedly published in the *Guardian* of June 19, 1878, under circumstances explained in a letter from the Rev. W. Benham to the Archbishop, which appeared in the *Guardian* of the following week, June 26, 1878, p. 900.

[2] Bishop of Grahamstown 1856–1871 ; Bishop of Edinburgh 1871–1886.

[3] The Rev. R. T. Davidson.

President, and that the memorialists should be informed that in no case could any answer be returned.]

In the opening debates during the first week the formal motion was in each case for the appointment of a Committee to consider the particular subject under discussion, and to report to the Conference during the closing week of Session. On the final and very wide subject—(No. VI.)—" The condition, progress, and needs of the various Churches of the Anglican Communion," the order was varied by the appointment of an influential Committee presided over by the Archbishop of Canterbury, which sat *de die in diem* at Lambeth, "to receive questions submitted in writing by Bishops desiring the advice of the Conference on difficulties or problems they have met with in their several Dioceses."

The various Committees met at Lambeth, Fulham, Farnham, and elsewhere during the fortnight which intervened between the first and last groups of Sessions, and their Reports were, for the most part, ready when the Conference re-assembled in Lambeth Library on Monday, July 22nd. On subject No. V. alone—" Modern forms of Infidelity, and the best means of dealing with them,"—the Committee, as was natural, announced that they had not found it possible to prepare in the time allotted for their deliberations a detailed Report upon so vast a question. To judge, however, from the published opinions of the Bishops present at the Conference[1] the debates upon this subject were among the most useful of any that took place.

As the outcome of much discussion it was decided that the Reports, when adopted by the Conference, should be incorporated as a whole in a combined

---

[1] See, for example, "The Second Lambeth Conference : A Personal Narrative," by Bishop Stevens Perry, of Iowa, pp. 27, &c.

"Letter," and put forth to the world in the name of the hundred Bishops assembled. This course was rendered possible by the almost complete unanimity with which the five Reports in their ultimate shape received the imprimatur of the Conference. Bishop Wordsworth of Lincoln, who, as Archdeacon of Westminster, had in 1867 translated into Greek and Latin the Address then published[1] undertook in like manner to make translations of this document of 1878, condensing or omitting such portions of the Reports as would be inappropriate or uninteresting to those outside the Anglican Communion.[2]

The final paragraphs of the official letter, which will be found in its complete form elsewhere,[3] were as follows :—

"These are the Reports of the Conference, and the practical conclusions at which we have arrived. Some of these conclusions have reference to the special circumstances of different branches of the One Church of Christ, according to peculiarities of their various missionary work for the heathen, or their labours among their own people ; some embody principles which apply to all branches of the Church Universal. They are all limited in their scope to those subjects which have been distinctly brought before the assembled Bishops. We invite to them the attention of the various Synods and other governing powers in the several Churches, and of all the faithful in Christ Jesus throughout the world.

"We do not claim to be lords over God's heritage, but we commend the results of this our Conference to the reason and conscience of our brethren as enlightened by the Holy Spirit of God, praying that all throughout the world who call upon the Lord Jesus Christ may be of one mind, may be united in

---

[1] See Part II., No. VII., p. 57.
[2] See Part II., No. XIX., p. 145.
[3] See Part II., No. XVIII., p. 117.

one fellowship, may hold fast the Faith once delivered to the Saints, and worship their one Lord in the spirit of purity and love.

" Signed on behalf of the Conference,

"A. C. CANTUAR."

The Letter having been thus formally signed, the *Gloria in Excelsis* was sung by the assembled Bishops, the Benediction was pronounced, and the deliberations of the Conference were at an end.

On the following day (Saturday, July 27) a grand closing service was held in St. Paul's Cathedral. The Bishops who were able to be present—about eighty-five in number—received the Archbishop of Canterbury at the West door, and the hymn, "The Church's One Foundation," was sung as the long procession walked up the nave. The *Te Deum*[1] followed, and the Holy Communion was then celebrated by the Archbishop of Canterbury, who was assisted in the service and administration by the Bishops of London, Moray and Ross, Sydney, Montreal, Christ Church (New Zealand), Capetown, Rupertsland, and Delaware. The sermon was preached by Bishop Stevens, of Pennsylvania, from the text, "I, if I be lifted up from the earth, will draw all men unto Me" (St. John xii. 32).[2] The service over, the Bishops assembled in the apse of the Cathedral, when a few farewell words were spoken by the Archbishop. "I feel confident," he said, "that the effect of our gathering will be that the Church at home and abroad will be strengthened by the mutual counsel which we have taken together. May the blessing of Almighty God, the Father, the Son, and the Holy Ghost attend each one of us in our several spheres when we depart from this place. On behalf of the Bishops

---

[1] Stainer in E flat.
[2] The sermon was published in pamphlet form by Messrs. Cassell & Co.

of England I offer to those of our brethren who have come hither from foreign lands our heartfelt thanks, and bid them, in the name of God, Farewell!"

So ended the second Lambeth Conference. It had been attended, as has been seen, by exactly one hundred Bishops. Thirty-five of these were English,[1] nine were Irish, seven were Scottish, thirty were Colonial and Missionary, and nineteen belonged to the Church of the United States. The expenses of the Conference, so far as they did not devolve upon the Archbishop of Canterbury, were defrayed by the English Diocesan Bishops. A committee of laymen, under the guidance of Mr. J. G. Talbot, M.P., undertook to arrange for all possible hospitality to the American and Colonial Bishops. This organization, however, as well as the visits paid to the English Universities and Cathedral cities, lay altogether outside the official arrangements for the Conference.[2]

The foregoing narrative has dealt simply with the two Conferences in their bare official aspect. The indirect results which have accrued are probably at least as great as those of an official kind. For an estimate of these indirect results, however, and for the impression made by the debates upon those who attended them, the reader must turn to the accounts which have been published in ample number in the biographies of Bishops on both sides of the Atlantic.[3]

In the twenty-one years that have elapsed between the first Conference and the third, the number of Bishops entitled to receive an invitation has increased

---

[1] Namely, two Archbishops, twenty-six English Diocesans, three Suffragan Bishops, and four ex-Colonial Bishops holding "permanent commissions" in England.

[2] For the numbers attending the Conference of 1867, see above, page 15.

[3] *e.g.* Lives of Bishops Sumner, Gray, Hopkins, Ewing, Selwyn, Kerfoot, Wilberforce, Wordsworth, &c.

from 144 to 209, and the relative increase is still greater in the number of those who have accepted the invitation to be present.[1] The keen interest and the high hopes expressed with regard to the Conference now about to open, under a third Archiepiscopal President, with a programme[2] at least as ample as those of 1867 and 1878, are evidence enough, were such required, that those who planned, in faith and courage, the first of these decennial gatherings, were right in believing that a solid gain must follow, and that not to the Anglican Communion only, but to the Church of Christ throughout the world.

June 1, 1888.

---

[1] The actual numbers are as follows :—

	Received Invitations.	Accepted the Invitation and Attended.
Conference of 1867 ...	144	76
,, ,, 1878 ...	173	100
,, ,, 1888 ...	209	? 143* * (Acceptances.)

[2] See Part II., No. XXII., p. 161.

PART II.—LETTERS AND DOCUMENTS ILLUSTRATING THE HISTORY OF THE LAMBETH CONFERENCES OF 1867 AND 1878.

No. I. (See page 6.)

Addresses from the Provincial Synod of the United Church of England and Ireland in Canada, assembled at Montreal in September, 1865; *with the Reply of the Archbishop of Canterbury.*

To the Most Reverend the Archbishop, the Right Reverend the Bishops, and the Reverend the Clergy of the Convocation of the Province of Canterbury.

We, the Bishops, Clergy, and Laity of the Canadian Branch of the United Church of England and Ireland, in Synod assembled, would approach your Venerable Body with the deepest sentiments of reverence and affection.

We are engaged, like yourselves, in endeavouring, in this distant dependency of the Crown, to uphold the truth of Religion, as our Common Church maintains it, and that Apostolic Order which is so essential a safeguard in the preservation and diffusion of the Catholic Faith. Recent declarations in high places in our Mother-land, in reference to the position of the Colonial Branches of the Mother Church, have created amongst us feelings of regret and apprehension, as tending to shake the conviction, always so dear to us, that we in the Colonies were, in all respects, one with the Church of our parent country.

No statute or decision, we beg solemnly to assure you, much as it may serve to weaken our outward connection with the Church of our fathers, can impair the integrity and vigour of those principles in doctrine and fellowship which constitute her inward life. We are one with her in the great Articles of Christian Belief, and one with her in that Episcopal Order which binds her members in unity throughout the world.

In desiring most earnestly to retain this connection, we believe that it would be most effectually preserved and perpetuated if means could be adopted by which the members of our Anglican Communion in all quarters of the world should have a share in the deliberations for her welfare, and be permitted to have a representation in one General Council of her members gathered from every land. Deeply affected by the threat of isolation which recent declarations in high places have indicated, we earnestly solicit this measure of relief, as maintaining that test of inward communion which is to us the most precious.

But while we look with hope to such concession, we readily affirm our belief that the manner and measure of the relief and encouragement we solicit will be left most wisely to the deliberate judgment of those ancient Convocations of the Church to whom, under God, the cause of true religion at home and abroad is so largely indebted.

Dated at the City of Montreal, in the Province of Canada, this twentieth day of September, in the year of our Lord one thousand eight hundred and sixty-five.

F. MONTREAL, JAMES BEAVEN, D.D.,
Metropolitan. *Prolocutor.*

To His Grace Charles Thomas, Archbishop of Canterbury, D.D., Primate of all England, and Metropolitan.

May it please your Grace,—

We, the Bishops, Clergy, and Laity of the Province of Canada, in Triennial Synod assembled, desire to represent to your Grace, that in consequence of the recent decisions of the Judicial Committee of the Privy Council in the well-known case respecting the *Essays and Reviews*, and also in the case of the Bishop of Natal and the Bishop of Cape Town, the minds of many members of the Church have been unsettled or painfully alarmed; and that doctrines hitherto believed to be Scriptural, and undoubtedly held by the members of the Church of England and Ireland, have been adjudicated upon by the Privy Council in such a way as to lead thousands of our brethren to conclude that, according to this decision, it is quite compatible with membership in the Church of England to discredit the historical facts of Holy Scripture, and to disbelieve the eternity of future punishment; moreover, we would express to your Grace the intense alarm felt by many in Canada lest the tendency of the revival of the active powers of Convocation should leave us governed by canons different from those in force in England and Ireland, and thus cause us to drift into the status of an independent branch of the Catholic Church—a result which we would at this time most solemnly deplore.

In order, therefore, to comfort the souls of the faithful, and reassure the minds of wavering members of the Church, and to obviate, as far as may be, the suspicion whereby so many are scandalised, that the Church is a creation of Parliament, we humbly entreat your Grace, since the assembling of a General Council of the whole Catholic Church is at present impracticable, to convene a National Synod of the Bishops of the Anglican Church at home and abroad, who, attended by one or more of their presbyters or laymen, learned in ecclesiastical law, as their advisers, may meet together, and, under the guidance of the Holy Ghost, take such counsel and adopt such measures as may be best fitted to provide for the present distress in such Synod, presided over by your Grace.

F. MONTREAL,   JAS. BEAVEN, D.D.,
Metropolitan, President.   *Prolocutor.*

Reply of the Archbishop.

To the Bishops, Clergy, and Laity of the Province of Canada, lately assembled in their Triennial Synod.

ADDINGTON PARK, *December*, 1865.

MY RIGHT REV., REV., AND DEAR BRETHREN,—

I have duly received the Address forwarded to me by your Metropolitan, from the late Triennial Provincial Synod of the Province of Canada, requesting me to convene a Synod of the Bishops of the Anglican Church, both at home and abroad, in order that they may meet together, and, under the guidance of the Holy Ghost, take such counsel, and adopt such measures, as may be best fitted to provide for the present distress.

I can well understand your surprise and alarm at the recent decisions of the Judicial Committee of the Privy Council in grave matters bearing upon the doctrine and discipline of our Church, and I can comprehend your anxiety, lest the recent revival of action in the two Provincial Convocations of Canterbury and York should lead to the disturbance of those relations, which have hitherto subsisted between the different branches of the Anglican Church.

The meeting of such a Synod as you propose is not by any means foreign to my own feelings, and I think it might tend to prevent those inconveniences, the possibility of which you anticipate. I cannot, however, take any step in so grave a matter without consulting my episcopal brethren in both branches of the United Church of England and Ireland, as well as those in the different colonies and dependencies of the British Empire.

I remain, your faithful and affectionate friend and brother in Christ,

C. T. CANTUAR,
Primate of All England.

No. II. (See page 6.)

Proceedings of the Convocation of Canterbury with respect to the Canadian Address of September, 1865.

On May 2, 1866, the Lower House unanimously resolved, "That his Grace the President be respectfully requested to direct the appointment of a Committee to consider and report upon the Address of the Canadian Branch of the United Church of England and Ireland, dated at Montreal, September 20, 1865."—(*Chronicle of Convocation*, May 2, 1866, p. 290.)

The President having granted this request, a Committee of fifteen members was appointed. The Committee presented its report on June 29, 1866, but the debate upon it was postponed until the following group of sessions.

On February 14, 1867, the Lower House, after a prolonged discussion, agreed by a majority of 29 to the following resolution :—

"That this House tenders its sincere thanks to the Committee on the Address of the Canadian Church, for the labour which they have bestowed on the subject, and for the Report which they have framed and presented to this House, and desires to convey to his Grace the Archbishop of Canterbury a respectful expression of an earnest desire that he would be pleased to issue an invitation to all the Bishops in communion with the Church of England to assemble at such time and place, and accompanied by such persons as may be deemed fit, for the purpose of Christian sympathy and mutual counsel on matters affecting the welfare of the Church at home and abroad ; and that this resolution be forwarded to the Upper House."

A debate upon the subject took place in the Upper House on the following day. No formal resolution was proposed, but the Archbishop announced his intention of acceding to the request which had been made.—(*Chronicle of Convocation, February* 14 and 15, 1867, *pp.* 767-793, 800-808.)

No. III. (See page 9.)

Official Programme for the Conference of 1867.

Arrangements for the Conference of Bishops of the Anglican Communion, to be holden at Lambeth Palace on September 24, 1867, and following days.

FIRST DAY.—Tuesday, September 24, at eleven o'clock, a.m. Prayers and Holy Communion. Sermon, by the Bishop of Illinois.

General Subject for the Day's Discussion.

INTERCOMMUNION BETWEEN THE CHURCHES OF THE ANGLICAN COMMUNION.

Opening Address of the President: specifying the general principles and rules of the Conference, and inviting any introductory remarks from Home Metropolitans and from distant Bishops.

General agreement as to the arrangement of the time and subjects.

Resolution :—

We, Bishops of Christ's Holy Catholic Church, professing the faith of the primitive and undivided Church, as based on Scripture, defined by the first four General Councils,[1] and reaffirmed by the Fathers of the English Reformation, now assembled by the good providence of God at the Archiepiscopal Palace of Lambeth, under the presidency of the Primate of all England, desire first to give hearty thanks to Almighty God for having thus brought us together for common counsels, and united worship; Secondly, we desire to express the deep sorrow with which we view the divided condition of the flock of Christ throughout the world; and, Lastly, we do here solemnly declare our belief that the best hope of future reunion will be found in drawing each of us for ourselves closer to our common Lord, in giving ourselves to much prayer and intercession, in the cultivation of a spirit of charity, and in seeking to diffuse through every part of the Christian community that desire and resolution to return to the faith and discipline of the undivided Church which was the principle of the English Reformation.

Resolution :—

Notification of New Sees and Bishops.

That it appears to us expedient, for the purpose of maintaining brotherly intercommunion, that all cases of establishment of new Sees, and appointment of new Bishops, be notified to all Archbishops and Metropolitans of the Home and Colonial Church

---

[1] See 1 Eliz., c. i. xxxvi.

of England and Ireland, the Primus of the Protestant Episcopal Church in Scotland, and the Presiding Bishop of the Protestant Episcopal Church in the United States of America.

Resolution :—

Letters Commendatory.

That, having regard to the conditions under which intercommunion between Members of the Church passing from one distant Diocese to another may be duly maintained, we hereby deem it desirable—

(1) That forms of Letters Commendatory on behalf of clergymen visiting other Dioceses be drawn up and agreed upon, and that no strange clergyman should officiate in any Diocese without exhibiting such Commendatory Letters to the Bishop thereof ;

(2) That a form of Letters Commendatory for such Laymen as may desire to avail themselves of them be in like manner prepared.

The Benediction.

SECOND DAY.—Wednesday, September 25.

General Subject for the Day's Discussion.

COLONIAL CHURCHES.

Resolution :—

Subordination to Metropolitans.

That it be a matter for the consideration of this Conference, and of the Bishops of the Colonial Church especially—

(1) Whether it be desirable that such Colonial and Missionary Dioceses as have not as yet been gathered into Provinces be formed into any Province; and

(2) Whether any, and if so what, steps should be taken.

Resolution :—

Discipline to be exercised by Metropolitans.

That, whereas schemes for conducting Ecclesiastical Affairs and for the exercising of Discipline have been embodied in the Letters Patent granted by the Crown to the Metropolitans of Canada, India, Australasia, New Zealand, and South Africa, it appears to us to be desirable that the aforesaid schemes so embodied in the Letters Patent be, for the present, and until the local authorities, spiritual and temporal, have otherwise provided, as much as possible adhered to; and that in all cases where the power of coercive jurisdiction is not conveyed by such Letters Patent it is desirable to provide by voluntary agreement for the enforcement of discipline, and that with a view to secure this end, all Bishops at their Consecration, and clergymen of those Dioceses at their ordination or institution to the cure of souls, should be required to pledge themselves to submit to the provisions of such schemes.

Resolution :—

Court of Metropolitans.

That in the case of any charges being preferred against a Suffragan Bishop of any Province, it appears to us desirable that the Metropolitan thereof should summon all the Bishops of his Province to sit with him for the hearing of the case, and that he should not proceed to the hearing of it without the aid and concurrence of all the Bishops of his Province that can be assembled.

The question of any charge being brought against a Metropolitan should also be considered.

Resolution :—

Question of Appeal.

That it be a matter for the consideration of this Conference whether, in cases where no Letters

Patent have been issued, any, and if any what, Appeal should lie from such Provincial Decisions.

Resolution :—

Conditions of Union.

That it be a matter for the consideration of this Conference, in reference to Colonial Churches not legally united to the United Churches of England and Ireland, what safeguards as to their continued soundness in Doctrine and Discipline be required by the Mother Church as the condition of the maintenance of full spiritual and ecclesiastical communion.

The Benediction.

THIRD DAY.—Thursday, September 26th.

General Subject for the Day's Discussion.

CO-OPERATION IN MISSIONARY ACTION.

Resolution :—

Notification of proposed Missionary Bishoprics.

That in case it should be proposed to found a Missionary Bishopric by any of the branches of the Church represented in this Conference, it seems to us desirable—

(1) That notification of such intention be sent to all Archbishops and Metropolitans of the Home and Colonial Church of England and Ireland, the Primus of the Protestant Episcopal Church in Scotland, and the Presiding Bishop of the Protestant Episcopal Church in the United States ; and

(2) That, so soon as any person is consecrated to such Bishopric, the announcement of such Consecration be made to the same parties.

Resolution :—

Subordination of Missionaries.

That, in the case of the establishment of any Missionary Bishopric, and consecration of a Bishop to the same, we deem it expedient that all Missionaries should place themselves under the general superintendence of such Missionary Bishop, subject always to their obedience to such written instructions as may be sent to them by those in authority at home.

Concluding resolution :—

That we desire to render our hearty thanks to Almighty God for the blessings vouchsafed to us in and by this Conference; and we desire to express our hope that this our Meeting may hereafter be followed by other Meetings to be conducted in the spirit of the same brotherly love.

The Closing Benediction.

No. IV. (See page 10.)

Opening Address delivered by the Archbishop of Canterbury in the first Session of the first Lambeth Conference, September 24, 1867.

My Most Reverend and Right Reverend Brethren,

In opening the proceedings of the first Conference that has ever taken place of the Bishops of the Reformed Church in visible communion with the United Church of England and Ireland, my prevailing feeling is one of profound gratitude to our Heavenly Father for having thus far prospered the efforts which have been made to promote this solemn assembling of ourselves together. Many have been the anxious thoughts and great the heart-searchings which have attended the preparations for this remarkable manifestation of life and energy in the several branches of our communion. Many also have been the prayers, and fervent, I trust, will continue to be the prayers, offered up by us, severally and collectively, that He will prosper our deliberations, to the advancement of His glory and the good of His Church. Having met together, as I truly believe we have done, in a spirit of love to Christ, and to all those who love Him, with an earnest desire to strengthen the bonds which unite the several branches of our Reformed Church, to encourage each other in our endeavours to maintain the faith once delivered to the saints, and to advance the kingdom of Christ upon earth, I will not doubt that a blessing from above will rest upon our labours, and that the guidance of the Holy Spirit, whose aid we have invoked, will direct, sanctify, and govern our counsels.

The origin of this Conference has already been stated in the circular of invitation which I addressed to you all. It was at the instance of the Metropolitan and the Bishops of the Church of Canada, supported by the unanimous request of a very large meeting of Archbishops and Bishops of the Home and Colonial Church—a request confirmed by addresses from both the Houses of Convocation of my Province of Canterbury—that I resolved upon convening it. Further encouragement to venture upon this unprecedented step was afforded when the petition from the Canadian Church was first discussed, a plain intimation being given by a distinguished member of the Protestant Episcopal Church in the United States of America, that it would be regarded as a very graceful act, and would be hailed with general satisfaction in that Church, if the invitation to the Conference were extended to our Episcopalian brethren in those States.

'Fully conscious, however, of all the difficulties which must surround the attempt to organise and superintend an assembly of so novel a character, I might well have hesitated to incur so great a risk; but to have refused to yield to wishes thus fully and forcibly expressed, to have shrunk from undertaking the consequent responsibility, would have been unworthy of the position in which, by God's providence, I am placed. In faith and prayer has the task been undertaken, and I humbly trust it will please God to prosper our work to a successful conclusion. The result, indeed, has thus far more than justified the expectations raised. We rejoice to find that so many of our brethren from distant parts of the globe have been moved to respond to the call, and we welcome with feelings of cordial affection and genuine sympathy the presence of so large a proportion of the American Episcopate. From very many also, who, owing to various circumstances, have been prevented from joining us, I have received letters expressing the profound satisfaction and thankfulness with which they regard the opportunities afforded by this gathering for conferring together upon topics of mutual interest; for discussing the peculiar difficulties and perplexities in which our widely-scattered Colonial Churches are involved, and the evils to which they are exposed; for cementing yet more firmly the bonds of Christian communion between Churches acknowledging one Lord, one faith, one baptism—connected not only by the ties of kindred, but by common formularies; and for meeting, through their representatives, from the most distant regions of the earth, to offer up united prayers and praise to the Most High in the mother tongue common to us all, and to partake together of the Holy Communion of the Body and Blood of our Saviour Christ.

It has never been contemplated that we should assume the functions of a General Synod of all the Churches in full communion with the Church of England, and take upon ourselves to enact canons that should be binding upon those here represented. We merely propose to discuss matters of practical interest, and pronounce what we deem expedient in resolutions which may serve as safe guides to future action. Thus it will be seen that our first essay is rather tentative and experimental, in a matter in which we have no distinct precedent to direct us.

The subjects which will be brought under your consideration have already been laid before you in the Prospectus of Arrangements for our proceedings. They may be briefly comprised under the following heads:—(1) The best way of promoting the Reunion of Christendom. (2) The Notification of the Establishment of New Sees. (3) Letters commendatory from Clergymen and Laymen passing to distant Dioceses. (4) Subordination in our Colonial Church to Metropolitans. (5) Discipline to be exercised by Metropolitans. (6) Court of the Metropolitan. (7) Question of Appeal. (8) Conditions of Union with the Church at home. (9) Notification of proposed Missionary Bishoprics. (10) Subordination of Missionaries. In the selection of topics regard has been chiefly had to those which bear on practical difficulties seeming to require solution. It has been found impossible to meet all views, and embrace every recommendation that has been suggested. Some may be of opinion that subjects have been omitted which ought to have found a place in our deliberations; that we should have been assembled with the view of defining the limits of Theological Truth; but it has been deemed far better, on the first occasion of our meeting in such form, rather to do too little than attempt too much, and instead of dealing with propositions which can lead to no efficient result, to confine ourselves to matters admitting of a practical and beneficial solution.

The unexpected position in which our Colonial Churches have recently found themselves placed has naturally created a great feeling of uneasiness in the minds of many. I am fully persuaded that the idea of any essential separation from the Mother Church is universally repudiated by them; they all cling to her with the strongest filial affection, while they are bound to her Doctrines and Form of Worship by cogent motives of interest. At the same time I have good reason to believe that there are various shades of opinion as to the best modes in which the connection between the daughter Churches and their common mother can be maintained; and I trust that the interchange of thought between those who are chiefly interested in those important questions will lead to some profitable conclusions. I may also state my belief that legislation on the subject of the Colonial Churches has been postponed until the view taken by this Conference shall have been declared. These matters have been regarded under various aspects in the voluminous correspondence which I have had with many of my Colonial brethren; they will all, no doubt, be fully developed in the course of our discussion by those who represent these several opinions. I trust that, under a deep sense of the solemnity of the occasion on which we are assembled, our discussions will be characterised by mutual forbearance, if sentiments at variance with our own shall be advanced, so that by the comparison, rather than the conflict of opinions, we may be drawn nearer to each other in brotherly harmony and concord. With the arrangement that certain subjects shall, after a brief consideration, be referred to Committees, I believe that the various topics for consideration may be profitably discussed.

Doubtless there is much in these latter days, even

as we have all been taught to expect, which is dark and dispiriting to the mind that has not been exercised to discern the meaning of such signs. The enemy is on every side, plying his insidious arts to sap the foundations of belief, to hinder the cause of God's Church, and prevent the Word of God from doing its work in the conversion of the soul of sinful man. No effort is spared to disparage the authority of those who witness for the truth and uphold the dogmatic teaching for which the Apostolic writings are at once the model and the warrant. Though it be not our purpose to enter upon theological discussion, yet our very presence here is a witness to our resolution to maintain the faith, which we hold in common as our priceless heritage, set forth in our Liturgy and other formularies; and this our united celebration of offices common to our respective Churches in each quarter of the globe is a claim, in the face of the world, for the independence of separate Churches, as well as a protest against the assumption by any Bishop of the Church Catholic of dominion over his fellows in the Episcopate.

Not one of us, I am persuaded, can fail to respond to that earnest desire for unity which is expressed in the introduction to our resolutions. It is but the echo of the petition which the Saviour of the world offered in behalf of His Church when He prayed the Father that those who should believe in Him might all be one in the Father and the Son. And while we deplore the divided state of Christendom, and mourn over the obstacles which at present exist to our all being joined together in the unity of the Spirit and in the bond of peace, this very feeling should be our most powerful motive to urge our petitions at the Throne of Grace, that it may please God, in His own good time, to remove such hindrances as at present render that union impracticable.

And now may our Almighty Father shed abroad upon us the spirit of wisdom, peace, and love, and inspire us with such counsels as may most tend to edification; so that, being knit together more closely in the bonds of brotherly affection and Christian communion, and animated with a more fervent zeal for the Saviour's honour and the salvation of souls, we may do our endeavour to prepare His Church for the coming of Him whom we lovingly adore, and whose advent in power and glory we ardently took to and long for.

No. V. (See page 12.)

Amended Programme adopted during the Sessions.

SECOND DAY.—Wednesday, September 25.

General Subject for the Day's Discussion.

COLONIAL CHURCHES.

Resolution I. :—

Alteration of Order.

That His Grace the President of this meeting be requested to allow the last Resolution headed "*Conditions of Union,*" to be first taken into consideration.

Resolution II. :—

Conditions of Union.

(*a*). That in the opinion of this Conference, "Unity in the Faith," and fellowship in the one Body of Christ, will be best maintained among the several branches of the Anglican Communion in the manner already pointed out by the Convocation of

Amended Programme, Sept. 25, 1867.

the Province of Canterbury: viz., by the due and Canonical subordination of the Synods of the several Branches to the higher authority of the Synods above them, the Diocesan Synod being recognised as inferior to the Provincial Synod, and the Provincial Synod to some higher Synod or Synods of the Anglican Communion.

Appointment of Committee.

(*b*). That a Committee of   members (with power to add to their number, and to obtain the assistance of men learned in Ecclesiastical and Canon Law) be appointed to inquire into and report upon the whole subject; and that such report be forwarded to His Grace the Lord Archbishop of Canterbury, with a request that, if possible, it may be communicated to any adjourned meeting of this Conference.

Proposed Inquiry into Disunion in Natal.

(*c*). That in the judgment of the Bishops now assembled, the whole Anglican Communion is deeply injured by the present condition of the Church in Natal; and that a Committee be now appointed at this General Meeting to consider the whole case, and inquire into all the proceedings which have been taken therein; and to report on the best mode by which the Church may be delivered from the continuance of this scandal, and the true faith maintained. That such Report be forwarded to his Grace the Lord Archbishop of Canterbury, with a request that, if possible, it may be communicated to any adjourned meeting of the Conference; and

Further, that his Grace be requested to transmit the same to all the Bishops[1] of the Anglican Communion, and to ask for their judgment thereupon.

---

[1] ? Convocations, Conventions, and Synods.

Resolution III. :—

Question of Appeal.

That in the opinion of this Conference, it is very desirable that there should be a Board of Reference, or a Spiritual Tribunal for final appeal and decision in all matters of Faith; including Representatives from all Branches of the Anglo-Catholic Church; and the Bishops here assembled earnestly recommend this most important matter to the deliberate consideration of the Convocations, Conventions, and Synods of the said Anglo-Catholic Church.

Or, if Resolution III. should not be carried, then—
Question of Appeal.

III. That in order to the maintenance of the strictest union between the Mother-Church of England and her daughter Churches in the Colonies, it is desirable that in questions of doctrine there should be an appeal from the tribunals for the exercise of Discipline in each Province to a spiritual tribunal in England.

That such tribunal be presided over by the Primate of all England (for the time being), and be composed of Bishops only.

Appointment of Committee.

And—

That a Committee be appointed to consider the details of the Constitution of such tribunal, and that their Report be forwarded to His Grace the Lord Archbishop of Canterbury, with a request that, if possible, it may be communicated to any adjourned meeting of the Conference.

Circulation of Report.

And further, that his Grace be requested to transmit the same to the Convocations and Synods of all the Provinces of the United Church of England and Ireland, and to all Bishops (if any) of the said Church not included in any Ecclesiastical Province.

Election of Members of Tribunal.

That His Grace the Archbishop of Canterbury be requested to invite the several Provinces of the Church to elect Bishops for the said Tribunal.

Resolution IV. :—

This Meeting to be followed by other Meetings.

That, in order to give effect to the above Resolutions, it is desirable that a General Synod of the Bishops of the Anglican Communion, accompanied, if it be thought fit, by other representatives from each Diocese, should be assembled from time to time under the Presidency of the Primate of all England.

Resolution V. :—

Time of First Meeting, &c.

That His Grace the Lord Archbishop is hereby requested to summon the First Meeting of such Synod for the year 187 ; and that in the opinion of this Conference the Primate of all England should be authorised to summon any Special Synod within that time, should the needs of the Church seem to require it; or should his Grace be requested to do so by   or more Bishops.

Conditions of Union.

Resolution VI. :—

That, in order to the binding of the Churches of our Colonial Empire and the Missionary Churches beyond them in the closest union with the Mother-Church, it is necessary that they receive and maintain without alteration the standards of Faith and Doctrine, as they are in use in that Church. That nevertheless each Province should have the right to make such adaptations and additions to the services of the Church as its peculiar circumstances may require.

Provided, That no change or addition be made inconsistent with the spirit and principles of the Book of Common Prayer, and that all such changes be liable to revision by any Synod of the Anglican Communion in which the said Province shall be represented.

Resolution VII. :—

Court of Metropolitans.

That in case of charges being brought against a Suffragan Bishop of any Province it appears to be desirable that the Metropolitan thereof should summon all the Bishops of his Province to sit with him for the hearing of the case, and that he should not proceed to the hearing of it without the aid of all the Bishops of the Province that can be assembled, who shall sit with him as judges.

That the question of any charge brought against a Metropolitan be referred to the Committee appointed by Resolution III.

Resolution VIII. :—

Scheme for conducting Election of Bishops, when not otherwise provided for.

That it is the opinion of this Conference that the election of a Bishop of any Colonial Diocese should be made by the Synod of the Diocese convened for that purpose, with liberty to delegate this power to others. But that no such election should be deemed canonically valid until it shall have been confirmed by the Bishops of the Province.

That the rules for the regulation of such elections be made by the Synods of the several Provinces.

Resolution IX. :—

Declaration of Submission to Regulations of Synods.

That all Bishops at their Consecration should be required to make a written Declaration of adhesion and submission to the regulations agreed upon by the General Synod of the Anglican Communion ; and that a form of such Declaration be prepared by the Committee appointed by Resolution III.

No. VI. (See page 13.)

Formal Address to the Faithful from the Bishops attending the Conference of 1867.

To the Faithful in Christ Jesus, the Priests and Deacons, and the Lay Members of the Church of Christ in Communion with the Anglican Branch of the Church Catholic,—

We the undersigned Bishops, gathered under the good providence of God for prayer and conference at Lambeth, pray for you that ye may obtain grace, mercy, and peace from God our Father, and from the Lord Jesus Christ our Saviour.

We give thanks to God, brethren beloved, for the faith in our Lord Jesus Christ, and the love towards the saints, which hath abounded amongst you ; and for the knowlege of Christ which through you hath been spread abroad amongst the most vigorous races of the earth ; and with one mouth we make our supplications to God, even the Father, that by the power of the Holy Ghost He would strengthen us with His might, to amend amongst us the things which are amiss, to supply the things which are lacking, and to reach forth unto higher measures of love and zeal in worshipping Him, and in making known His name; and we pray that in His good time He would give back unto His whole Church the Blessed gift of Unity in Truth.

And now we exhort you in love that ye keep whole and undefiled the faith once delivered to the saints, as ye have received it of the Lord Jesus. We entreat you to watch and pray, and to strive heartily with us against the frauds and subtleties wherewith the faith hath been aforetime and is now assailed.

We beseech you to hold fast, as the sure word of God, all the canonical Scriptures of the Old and New Testament; and that by diligent study of these oracles of God, praying in the Holy Ghost, ye seek to know more of the Lord Jesus Christ our Saviour, very God and very Man, ever to be adored and worshipped, whom they reveal unto us, and of the will of God, which they declare.

Furthermore, we entreat you to guard yourselves and yours against the growing superstitions and additions with which in these latter days the truth of God hath been overlaid; as otherwise, so especially by the pretension to universal sovereignty over God's heritage asserted for the See of Rome, and by the practical exaltation of the Blessed Virgin Mary as mediator in the place of her Divine Son, and by the addressing of prayers to her as intercessor between God and man. Of such beware, we beseech you, knowing that the jealous God giveth not His honour to another.

Build yourselves up, therefore, beloved, in your most holy faith; grow in grace and in the knowledge and love of Jesus Christ our Lord. Show forth before all men by your faith, self-denial, purity, and godly conversation, as well as by your labours for the people amongst whom God hath so widely spread you, and by the setting forth of His Gospel to the unbelievers and the heathen, that ye are indeed the servants of Him who died for us to reconcile His Father to us, and to be a sacrifice for the sins of the whole world.

Brethren beloved, with one voice we warn you: the time is short; the Lord cometh; watch and be sober. Abide stedfast in the Communion of Saints, wherein God hath granted you a place. Seek in faith for oneness with Christ in the blessed Sacrament of His body and blood. Hold fast the Creeds and the pure worship and order, which of God's grace ye have inherited from the Primitive Church. Beware of causing divisions contrary to the doctrine ye have received. Pray and seek for unity amongst yourselves, and amongst all the faithful in Christ Jesus! and the good Lord make you perfect, and keep your bodies, souls, and spirits, until the coming of the Lord Jesus Christ.

(Signed)

C. T. Cantuar.
M. G. Armagh.
R. C. Dublin.
A. C. London.
C. R. Winton.
C. St. David's.
J. Lichfield.
S. Oxon.
Thomas Vowler St. Asaph.
A. Llandaff.
John Lincoln.
W. K. Sarum.
John T. Norwich.
J. C. Bangor.
H. Worcester.
Charles Wordsworth, D.C.L., Bishop of St. Andrew's, Dunkeld, and Dumblane.
Thos. G. Suther, Bishop of Aberdeen and Orkney.
William S. Wilson, Bishop of Glasgow and Galloway.
Thomas B. Morrell, Coadjutor Bishop of Edinburgh.
F. Montreal, Metropolitan of Canada.
G. A. New Zealand, Metropolitan of New Zealand.
R. Capetown, Metropolitan of South Africa.
Aubrey G. Jamaica.
T. Barbados.
J. Bombay.
H. Nova Scotia.
F. T. Labuan.
H. Grahamstown.
H. J. C. Christchurch.
Mathew Perth.
Benj. Huron.
W. W. Antigua.
E. H. Sierra Leone.
T. N. Honolulu.
J. T. Ontario.

J. W. Quebec.
W. J. Gibraltar.
H. L. Dunedin.
Edward, Bishop Orange River Free State.
A. N. Niagara.
William George Tozer, Missionary Bishop.
James B. Kelly, Coadjutor of Newfoundland.
S. Angl. Hierosol.

John H. Hopkins, Presiding Bishop of Pr. Ep. Church, in the United States.
Chas. P. McIlvaine, Bishop of Ohio.
G. J. Gloucester and Bristol.
E. H. Ely.
William Chester.
T. L. Rochester.
Horace Sodor and Mann.
Samuel Meath.
H. Kilmore.
Charles Limerick Ardfert and Aghadoe.

Robert Eden, D.D., Bishop of Moray, Ross, and Caithness, Primus.
Alexander Ewing, Bishop of Argyll and the Isles.
Manton Eastburn, Bishop of Massachusetts.
J. Payne, Bishop of Cape Palmas and parts adjacent.
H. J. Whitehouse, Bishop of Illinois.

Thomas Atkinson, Bishop of North Carolina.
Henry W. Lee, Bishop of Iowa.
Horatio Potter, Bishop of New York.
Thomas M. Clark, Bishop of Rhode Island.
Alexander Gregg, Bishop of Texas.
W. H. Odenheimer, Bishop of New Jersey.
G. T. Bedell, Assistant Bishop of Ohio.
Henry C. Lay, Missionary Bishop of Arkansas and the Indian Territory.
Jos. C. Talbot, Assistant Bishop of Indiana.
Richard H. Wilmer, Bishop of Alabama.
Charles Todd Quintard, Bishop of Tennessee.
John B. Kerfoot, Bishop of Pittsburgh.
J. P. B. Wilmer, Bishop of Louisiana.
C. M. Williams, Missionary Bishop to China.
J. Chapman, Bishop.
George Smith, late Bishop of Victoria (China).
David Anderson, late Bishop of Rupert's Land.
Edmund Hobhouse, by Bishop of New Zealand.

No. VII. (See page 28.)

LATIN AND GREEK VERSIONS OF THE ADDRESS.

Archdeacon Wordsworth, afterwards Bishop of Lincoln, translated the Episcopal Address into Latin and Greek, as follows :—

EPISTOLA ENCYCLICA.

EPISCOPORUM IN ANGLIA CONGREGATORUM DIEBUS XXIV.—XXVII MENSIS SEPTEMBRIS, ANNO SALUTIS MDCCCLXVII.

Fidelibus in Christo Jesu, Presbyteris, Diaconis, et Laicis, cum Anglicanâ parte Ecclesiæ Catholicæ communicantibus, salutem in Domino.

Nos, qui subscripsimus, Episcopi, benignâ Dei providentiâ communium orationum et consiliorum causâ unanimiter consociati, in Palatio Archiepiscopi Cantuariensis Lambethano, obsecrationes pro vobis facimus, ut gratiam, misericordiam et pacem consequamini a Deo Patre Nostro, et a Nostro Salvatore Domino Jesu Christo.

Gratias Deo agimus, fratres carissimi, propter fidem in Domino Jesu Christo, et in sanctos dilectionem, quæ abundavit in vobis; et propter Christi agnitionem, quæ per vos inter valentissimas orbis universi nationes dimanavit ; et uno ore supplicationes offerimus Deo et Patri, ut potentia Spiritûs Sancti virtute Suâ nos confortet, ut, quæ sint apud nos depravata, emendare, et, quæ desint, supplere valeamus; et ut nosmet ipsos ad sublimiores dilectionis et zeli mensuras erigamus in Illo adorando, et in Nomine Ejus declarando ; et enixè Eum apprecamur, ut, beneplacito Ipsius tempore, universæ Suæ Ecclesiæ beatum restituat donum Unitatis in Veritate.

Jam verò, fratres dilecti, vos in caritate cohortamur, ut fidem semel sanctis traditam integram atque illibatam conservetis, quemadmodum eam accepistis a Jesu Christo Domino Nostro. Obsecramus vos, vigilate, orate, et nobiscum toto corde certate contra fallacias atque argutias, quibus jampridem et in hoc ipso tempore fides impugnatur.

Obtestamur vos, constanter tenete, utpote firmum Dei Verbum, omnes Canonicas Scripturas Veteris et Novi Testamenti; et diligenti meditatione scrutantes hæc Dei Oracula, orantes in Spiritu Sancto, quæratis abundantiùs cognoscere Dominum Jesum Christum, Verum Deum et Verum Hominem, semper colendum atque adorandum, Quem nobis illa revelant, et Voluntatem Dei in eis patefactam.

Insuper vos obsecramus, vosmet ipsos et vestros custodite contra indies gliscentes superstitiones atque additamenta quibus in hisce novissimis temporibus Veritas Dei incrustatur; quùm in aliis, tùm præcipuè per universi principatûs affectationem dominantis in clero Dei, qui Romanæ sedi a nonnullis asseritur; et per exaltationem, re ipsâ manifestam, Beatæ Virginis Mariæ in locum Mediatoris, vice Filii ipsius Divini, et per orationes ei oblatas tanquam inter Deum et homines Interpellatoris munere fungenti. Cavete a talibus, vos obtestamur, probè scientes honorem Suum Ipsius non alii dare Deum zelotem.

Superædificamini, igitur, fratres carissimi, sanctissimæ fidei vestræ; crescite in gratiâ et in agnitione et dilectione Jesu Christi Domini Nostri. Manifestum facite omnibus, per fidem, abstinentiam, puritatem et sanctum conversationem, et per vestros labores pro populis inter quos Deus vos tam latè propagavit, et per Evangelii prædicationem incredulis atque ethnicis, vos reverâ esse servos Illius Qui mortuus est pro nobis ut Patrem nobis reconciliaret, et ut pro peccatis totius mundi sacrificium Semet Ipsum offerret.

Fratres dilecti, unâ voce vos admonemus. Tempus

breve est. Dominus venit. Vigilate, sobrii estote. State firmi in communione sanctorum in quâ vobis Deus locum concessit. Studete fide coadunari Christo in sanctissimo Corporis Ejus et Sanguinis Sacramento. Firma tenete Symbola, et purum illum Cultum atque Ordinem, quem gratià Dei a primitivâ Ecclesiâ hæreditarium vos possidetis. Cavete ne discessiones faciatis præter doctrinam quam accepistis. Orate et sectamini Unitatem invicem et inter omnes fideles in Jesu Christo. Et Dominus misericors perficiat vos, et conservet integrum corpus, animam et spiritum vestrum in Adventum Domini Nostri Jesu Christi. Amen.

    C. T. Cantuar. Archiepiscopus, et Metropolitanus, et totius Angliæ Primas.

    M. G. Armagh. Archiepiscopus, et Metropolitanus, et totius Hiberniæ Primas.

    R. C. Dublin. Archiepiscopus, et Metropolitanus, et Hiberniæ Primas.

    A. C. London. Episcopus.

    Robert Eden, Moray, Ross, Caithness. Episcopus, et Scoticæ Ecclesiæ Primas, &c. &c.

ΕΓΚΥΚΛΙΟΣ ΕΠΙΣΤΟΛΗ.

Ἐπισκόπων ἐν Ἀγγλίᾳ συνηθροισμένων, ἐν ἡμέραις 24—27 μηνὸς Σεπτεμβρίου, ἔτει 1867.

Τοῖς πιστοῖς ἐν Χριστῷ Ἰησοῦ, Πρεσβυτέροις, Διακόνοις καὶ λαϊκοῖς τῆς τοῦ Χριστοῦ Ἐκκλησίας, συγκοινωνοῖς τοῦ Ἀγγλικοῦ μέρους τῆς Καθολικῆς Ἐκκλησίας, χαίρειν ἐν Κυρίῳ.

Ἡμεῖς οἱ ὑπογράψαντες Ἐπίσκοποι, τῇ ἀγαθῇ τοῦ Θεοῦ προνοίᾳ ὁμοθυμαδὸν ἐπισυνηγμένοι, κοινῶν προσευχῶν ἕνεκα καὶ συμβουλεύσεως, ἐν τῷ τῆς Καντουαρίας Ἀρχιεπισκόπου παλατίῳ Λαμβηθανῷ, δεόμεθα ὑπὲρ ὑμῶν ἵνα λάβητε χάριν, ἔλεος, καὶ εἰρήνην ἀπὸ Θεοῦ

Πατρὸς, καὶ τοῦ Κυρίου ἡμῶν καὶ Σωτῆρος Ἰησου Χριστοῦ.

Εὐχαριστοῦμεν τῷ Θεῷ, ἀδελφοὶ ἀγαπητοὶ, ὑπὲρ τῆς πίστεως ὑμῶν ἐν Κυρίῳ ἡμῶν Ἰησοῦ Χριστῷ, καὶ ὑπὲρ τῆς ἀγάπης εἰς τοὺς ἁγίους, ἥτις ἐπερίσσευσεν ἐν ὑμῖν, καὶ ὑπὲρ τῆς Χριστοῦ ἐπιγνώσεως, ἣ δι᾽ ὑμῶν ἐξήχηται ἐν τοῖς ἀνδρειοτάτοις τῆς οἰκουμένης ἔθνεσιν· καὶ ἑνὶ στόματι δεήσεις ποιούμεθα πρὸς τὸν Θεὸν καὶ Πατέρα, ἵνα τῇ τοῦ Ἁγίου Πνεύματος δυνάμει σθενώσῃ ἡμᾶς τῇ ἰσχύι Αὐτοῦ, εἰς τὸ ἐπανορθῶσαι τὰ παραπίπτοντα, καὶ τὰ λείποντα ἀναπληρῶσαι, καὶ ἐπεκτείνεσθαι εἰς ὑψηλότερα ἀγάπης μέτρα καὶ ζήλου ἐν τῷ λατρεύειν αὐτῷ, καὶ ἐν τῷ γνωρίζειν τὸ ὄνομα αὐτοῦ· καὶ προσευχόμεθα ἵνα ἐν τῷ δεκτῷ αὐτοῦ καιρῷ ἀποδῷ τῇ ὅλῃ Αὐτοῦ ἐκκλησίᾳ τὸ μακαριστὸν χάρισμα τῆς ἑνότητος ἐν τῇ ἀληθείᾳ.

Καὶ νῦν, ἀδελφοὶ, παρακαλοῦμεν ὑμᾶς ἐν ἀγάπῃ, ἵνα τηρῆτε ὁλόκληρον καὶ ἀδιάφθορον τὴν ἅπαξ παραδοθεῖσαν τοῖς ἁγίοις πίστιν, καθὼς αὐτὴν παρειλήφατε ἀπὸ τοῦ Κυρίου Ἰησοῦ. Ἐρωτῶμεν ὑμᾶς ἵνα γρηγορῆτε καὶ προσεύχησθε, καὶ ἀγωνίζησθε εὐκαρδίως μεθ᾽ ἡμῶν κατὰ τῶν πανουργιῶν καὶ μεθοδειῶν, δι᾽ ὧν ἡ πίστις τὸ πρὶν καὶ ἐν τῷ νῦν παρόντι χρόνῳ πορθεῖται.

Παρακαλοῦμεν ὑμᾶς ἵνα ἀσφαλῶς κρατῆτε, ὡς βέβαιον Θεοῦ λόγον, πάσας τὰς κανονικὰς γραφὰς τῆς Παλαιᾶς καὶ τῆς Καινῆς Διαθήκης, καὶ ἵνα, σπουδαίως ἐρευνῶντες ταῦτα τὰ λόγια τοῦ Θεοῦ, ζητῆτε περισσοτέρως γνῶναι τὸν Κύριον καὶ Σωτῆρα Ἰησοῦν Χριστόν, Θεὸν ἀληθινὸν καὶ ἄνθρωπον ἀληθινὸν, ᾧ πάντοτε προσκυνεῖν δεῖ καὶ λατρεύειν, ὃν αἱ γραφαὶ ἡμῖν ἀνακαλύπτουσιν, καὶ τὸ θέλημα τοῦ Θεοῦ, τὸ ἐν αὐταῖς φανερούμενον.

Ἅμα δὲ ὑμῖν, ἀδελφοὶ, διαμαρτυρόμεθα, φυλάξατε ἑαυτοὺς καὶ τοὺς ὑμετέρους ἀπὸ τῶν ἀεὶ αὐξανομένων ἐθελοθρησκειῶν καὶ ἐπιβλημάτων, δι᾽ ὧν ἡ τοῦ Θεοῦ ἀλήθεια ἐν τοῖς ὑστέροις τούτοις χρόνοις παραπέπλασται, ἄλλως τε καὶ μάλιστα διὰ τῆς ἀντιποιήσεως μοναρχίας οἰκουμενικῆς, κατακυριευούσης τοῦ κλήρου τοῦ Θεοῦ, ἧς ἀξιοῦται παρά τισιν ἡ Ῥώμης καθέδρα· ἔτι δὲ διὰ τῆς ἐνεργοῦ ὑπεράρσεως τῆς μακαρίας Παρθένου Μαρίας εἰς τόπον Μεσίτου, ἀντὶ τοῦ Υἱοῦ αὐτῆς αὐτοθέου, καὶ διὰ προσευχῶν αὐτῇ προσφερομένων ὡς ἐντυγχανούσῃ ὑπὲρ ἀνθρώπων παρὰ Θεῷ. Προσέχετε ἀπὸ τοιούτων, εἰδότες ὅτι τὴν τιμὴν ἑαυτοῦ οὐχ ἑτέρῳ δίδωσιν ὁ ζηλωτὴς Θεός.

Ἐποικοδομεῖσθε οὖν, ἀγαπητοί, ἐπὶ τῇ ἁγιωτάτῃ ὑμῶν πίστει· αὐξάνεσθε ἐν χάριτι καὶ γνώσει καὶ ἀγάπῃ τοῦ Κυρίου ἡμῶν Ἰησοῦ Χριστοῦ. Καταδείξατε ἐνώπιον πάντων, διὰ τῆς πίστεως, αὐταπαρνήσεως, ἁγνείας, καὶ εὐσεβοῦς ἀναστροφῆς, ἅμα δὲ διὰ τῶν ὑμετέρων κόπων ὑπὲρ τῶν λαῶν ἐν οἷς ὁ Θεὸς ὑμᾶς εἰς τοσοῦτον εὖρος διαπεφύτευκε, καὶ διὰ τοῦ κηρύγματος τοῦ εὐαγγελίου τοῖς ἀπίστοις καὶ τοῖς ἔθνεσιν, ὅτι τῷ ὄντι ἐστὲ δοῦλοι Ἐκείνου, ὃς ἀπέθανεν ὑπὲρ ἡμῶν, ἵνα καταλλάξῃ ἡμῖν τὸν Πατέρα, καὶ ἵνα θυσίαν Ἑαυτὸν ἀνενέγκῃ ὑπὲρ τῶν ἁμαρτιῶν ὅλου τοῦ κόσμου.

Ἀδελφοὶ ἀγαπητοί, μιᾷ φωνῇ νουθετοῦμεν ὑμᾶς· ὁ καιρὸς συνεσταλμένος· ὁ Κύριος ἔρχεται· γρηγορεῖτε, νήφετε. Στήκετε ἑδραῖοι ἐν τῇ κοινωνίᾳ τῶν ἁγίων, ἐν ᾗ Θεὸς ὑμῖν μερίδα κεχάρισται· ζητεῖτε ἐν πίστει ἑνοῦσθαι τῷ Χριστῷ ἐν τῷ εὐλογημένῳ μυστηρίῳ τοῦ σώματος Αὐτοῦ καὶ αἵματος. Κατέχετε στερεῶς τὰ Σύμβολα, καὶ τὴν καθαρὰν θρησκείαν καὶ τάξιν, ἣν χάριτι Θεοῦ κεκληρονομήκατε ἀπὸ τῆς ἀρχῆθεν ἐκκλησίας. Βλέπετε μὴ διχοστασίας ποιῆτε κατὰ τῆς διδαχῆς ἣν ἐμάθετε. Ἐρωτᾶτε καὶ διώκετε ἑνότητα ἐν ἑαυτοῖς, καὶ ἐν πᾶσι τοῖς πιστοῖς ἐν Χριστῷ Ἰησοῦ· καὶ ὁ χρηστὸς Κύριος τελειώσαι ὑμᾶς, καὶ τηρῆσαι ὑμῶν τὸ σῶμα, τὴν ψυχὴν, καὶ τὸ πνεῦμα, εἰς τὴν παρουσίαν τοῦ Κυρίου Ἰησοῦ. Ἀμήν.

C. T. CANTUAR. ἀρχιεπίσκοπος, καὶ μητροπολίτης, καὶ πρῶτος ὅλης τῆς Ἀγγλίας.
M. G. ARMAGH. ἀρχιεπίσκοπος, καὶ μητροπολίτης, καὶ πρῶτος ὅλης τῆς Ἰβερνίας.
R. C. DUBLIN. ἀρχιεπίσκοπος, καὶ μητρcπολίτης, καὶ πρῶτος Ἰβερνίας.
A. C. LONDON. ἐπίσκοπος.
C. R. WINTON. ἐπίσκοπος.
κ.τ.λ.

No. VIII. (See page 13.)

The Formal Resolutions of the Conference of Sept. 24–27, 1867.

INTRODUCTION.

" We, Bishops of Christ's Holy Catholic Church in visible Communion with the United Church of England and Ireland, professing the Faith delivered to us in Holy Scripture, maintained by the Primitive Church and by the Fathers of the English Reformation, now assembled, by the good providence of God, at the Archiepiscopal Palace of Lambeth, under the presidency of the Primate of all England, desire —*First*, to give hearty thanks to Almighty God for having thus brought us together for common counsels and united worship ; *Secondly*, we desire to express the deep sorrow with which we view the divided condition of the flock of Christ throughout the world, ardently longing for the fulfilment of the prayer of our Lord, ' That all may be one, as Thou, Father, art in Me, and I in Thee, that they also may be one in us, that the world may believe that Thou hast sent Me ;' and, *Lastly*, we do here solemnly record our conviction that unity will be most effectually promoted by maintaining the Faith in its purity and integrity—as taught in the Holy Scriptures, held by the Primitive Church, summed up in the Creeds, and affirmed by the undisputed General Councils,—and by drawing each of us closer to our common Lord, by giving ourselves to much prayer and intercession, by the cultivation of a spirit of charity, and a love of the Lord's appearing."

Resolution I.—" That it appears to us expedient, for the purpose of maintaining brotherly intercommunion, that all cases of establishment of new Sees, and appointment of new Bishops, be notified to all

Archbishops and Metropolitans, and all presiding Bishops of the Anglican Communion."

Resolution II.—" That, having regard to the conditions under which intercommunion between members of the Church passing from one distant Diocese to another may be duly maintained, we hereby declare it desirable,—

"(1) That forms of Letters Commendatory on behalf of Clergymen visiting other Dioceses be drawn up and agreed upon ;

"(2) That a form of Letters Commendatory for lay members of the Church be in like manner prepared ;

"(3) That his Grace the Lord Archbishop of Canterbury be pleased to undertake the preparation of such forms."

Resolution III.—" That a Committee be appointed to draw up a Pastoral Address to all members of the Church of Christ in communion with the Anglican Branch of the Church Catholic, to be agreed upon by the assembled Bishops, and to be published as soon as possible after the last sitting of the Conference."

Resolution IV.—" That, in the opinion of this Conference, Unity in Faith and Discipline will be best maintained among the several branches of the Anglican Communion by due and canonical subordination of the Synods of the several branches to the higher authority of a Synod or Synods above them."

Resolution V.—" That a Committee of seven members (with power to add to their number, and to obtain the assistance of men learned in Ecclesiastical and Canon Law) be appointed to inquire into and report upon the subject of the relations and functions of such Synods, and that such Report be forwarded to his Grace the Lord Archbishop of Canterbury, with a request that, if possible, it may be communicated to any adjourned meeting of this Conference."

Resolution VI.—" That, in the judgment of the Bishops now assembled, the whole Anglican Communion is deeply injured by the present condition of the Church in Natal ; and that a Committee be now appointed at this General Meeting to report on the best mode by which the Church may be delivered from the continuance of this scandal, and the true faith maintained. That such Report be forwarded to his Grace the Lord Archbishop of Canterbury, with the request that he will be pleased to transmit the same to all the Bishops of the Anglican Communion, and to ask for their judgment thereupon."

Resolution VII.—" That we who are here present do acquiesce in the Resolution of the Convocation of Canterbury, passed on June 29, 1866, relating to the Diocese of Natal, to wit—

"'If it be decided that a new Bishop should be consecrated,—As to the proper steps to be taken by the members of the Church in the province of Natal for obtaining a new Bishop, it is the opinion of this House,—*first*, that a formal instrument, declaratory of the doctrine and discipline of the Church of South Africa should be prepared, which every Bishop, Priest, and Deacon to be appointed to office should be required to subscribe ; *secondly*, that a godly and well-learned man should be chosen by the clergy, with the assent of the lay-communicants of the Church; and, *thirdly*, that he should be presented for consecration, either to the Archbishop of Canterbury,—if the aforesaid instrument should declare the doctrine and discipline of Christ as received by the United Church of England and Ireland,—or to the Bishops of the Church of South Africa, according as hereafter may be judged to be most advisable and convenient.'"

Resolution VIII.—" That, in order to the binding of the Churches of our Colonial Empire and the Missionary Churches beyond them in the closest union with the Mother-Church, it is necessary that they receive and maintain without alteration the standards of Faith and Doctrine as now in use in that Church. That, nevertheless, each Province should have the right to make such adaptations and additions to the services of the Church as its peculiar circumstances may require. *Provided,* that no change or addition be made inconsistent with the spirit and principles of the Book of Common Prayer, and that all such changes be liable to revision by any Synod of the Anglican Communion in which the said Province shall be represented."

Resolution IX.—" That the Committee appointed by Resolution V., with the addition of the names of the Bishops of London, St. David's, and Oxford, and all the Colonial Bishops, be instructed to consider the constitution of a voluntary spiritual tribunal, to which questions of doctrine may be carried by appeal from the tribunals for the exercise of discipline in each Province of the Colonial Church, and that their report be forwarded to his Grace the Lord Archbishop of Canterbury, who is requested to communicate it to an adjourned meeting of this Conference."

Resolution X.—" That the resolutions submitted to this Conference relative to the discipline to be exercised by Metropolitans, the Court of Metropolitans, the scheme for conducting the Election of Bishops, when not otherwise provided for, the declaration of submission to the Regulation of Synods, and the question of what Legislation should be proposed for the Colonial Churches, be referred to the Committee specified in the preceding Resolution."

Resolution XI.—" That a special committee be appointed to consider the Resolutions relative to the notification of proposed Missionary Bishoprics, and the Subordination of Missionaries."

Resolution XII.—" That the question of the bounds of the jurisdiction of different Bishops, when any question may have arisen in regard to them, the question as to the obedience of Chaplains of the United Church of England and Ireland on the Continent, and the Resolution submitted to the Conference relative to their return and admission into Home Dioceses, be referred to the Committee specified in the preceding Resolution."

Resolution XIII.—" That we desire to render our hearty thanks to Almighty God for the blessings vouchsafed to us in and by this Conference; and we desire to express our hope that this our meeting may hereafter be followed by other meetings to be conducted in the same spirit of brotherly love."

No. IX. (See page 14.)

Correspondence with the Dean of Westminster respecting the use of Westminster Abbey in connection with the Conference of 1867.

1. *The Dean of Westminster to the Archbishop of Canterbury.*

DEANERY, WESTMINSTER,
September 21, 1867.

MY DEAR LORD ARCHBISHOP,

I have been honoured with a communication from your Grace, through the Bishop of London, requesting the use of Westminster Abbey for a special service to be held for the English, American, and Scottish Bishops now assembled in England, to be held, as I understood, on September 28.

On all occasions it is my earnest desire to render the Abbey and the precincts of Westminster available for purposes of general utility and edification, and this desire is increased when the request comes from your Grace.

You will kindly allow me to state the difficulty

which I feel in the present instance. I have endeavoured to act in such matters on the rule of granting the use of the Abbey to such purposes, and such only, as are either co-extensive with the Church of England, or have a definite object of usefulness or charity, apart from party or polemical considerations.

Your Grace will, I am sure, see that, however much your Grace's intentions would have brought the proposed Conference at Lambeth within this sphere, in fact, it can hardly be so considered. The absence of the Primate and the larger part of the Bishops of the Northern Province—not to speak of the Bishops of India and Australia, and of other important Colonial or Missionary Sees—must, even irrespectively of other indications, cause it to present a partial aspect of the English Church; whilst the appearance of other prelates not belonging to our Church, places it on a different footing from the institutions which are confined to the Church of England. And, further, the absence of any fixed information as to the objects to be discussed and promoted by the Conference, leaves me, in common with all who stand outside, in uncertainty as to what would be the proposals or measures which would receive, by implication, the sanction given by the use of the Abbey—a sanction which, in the case of a church so venerable and national in its character, ought, I conceive, to be lent only to public objects of well-defined or acknowledged beneficence.

These are the grounds why I hesitate to take upon myself the responsibility suggested. But, when stating this difficulty, I feel so strongly the value of the friendly intercourse to promote which has been the chief intention of your Grace, and of, I doubt not, many of the prelates who have concurred in this Conference; and I am so desirous that the Abbey should be made to minister to the edification of large sections of our Church, even when not representing the whole, and of those outside our own immediate pale (especially our brethren from America), who are willing to co-operate with us in all things lawful and good—that I would gladly, if possible, join in advancing such a purpose.

It has occurred to me, that, as the service indicated by your Grace is to be held after the Conference is finished, the Abbey might be granted for it, without any relation to the Conference itself; but either for some specific object, such as the Society for the Propagation of the Gospel, or for other Home or Foreign Missions of unquestioned importance, or else (in those general terms which, as I apprehend, express your Grace's wishes) for the promotion of brotherly goodwill and mutual edification amongst all members of the Anglican Communion.

Under these circumstances, and on this understanding, which I should wish to be made as public as the announcement of the service itself, I should have great pleasure in the permitting the use of the Abbey for such a service, to be held in the morning or afternoon of September 28th (as may be deemed most convenient), and I trust that, if this meets your Grace's wishes, your Grace will undertake to preach on the occasion.

I beg to remain, my dear Lord Archbishop,

Yours faithfully and respectfully,

A. P. STANLEY.

2. *The Archbishop of Canterbury to the Dean of Westminster.*

ADDINGTON PARK, CROYDON,
September 25, 1867.

MY DEAR DEAN,

I laid your note before the Conference yesterday, but it will probably not close its sittings on Friday evening, as there is reason to believe that committees will be appointed to report at a future date. Under these circumstances, it is obvious, from the tenor of your letter, that the Abbey is not open to us. I regret, therefore, that we shall not be able to avail ourselves of your kind offer, under the specified conditions.

Believe me, my dear Dean,
Yours very truly,
C. T. CANTUAR.

3. *The Dean of Westminster to the Archbishop of Canterbury.*

DEANERY, WESTMINSTER,
September 27, 1867.

MY DEAR LORD ARCHBISHOP,

I have to acknowledge, with thanks, your Grace's letter of the 25th, and to express my regret that your Grace and the Bishops assembled should have felt themselves precluded from accepting my proposal —in reply to your Grace's request—to meet in the Abbey for "some specific object of charity or usefulness," or for the purpose of promoting brotherly goodwill and mutual edification amongst all members of the Anglican Communion.

I beg, however, that you will assure the prelates assembled, especially those of our American brethren, for whose sake, as I stated in my former letter, I especially proposed to grant the use of the Abbey as before mentioned; that if they, or any of them should wish to attend the services in the Abbey on Sunday next (at 10 a.m. or at 3 p.m.) every accommodation and welcome shall be afforded.

I beg to remain, my dear Lord Archbishop,
Yours faithfully and respectfully,
A. P. STANLEY.

4. *The Dean of Westminster to the Bishop of Vermont, Presiding Bishop of the American Church.*

DEANERY, WESTMINSTER,
October 1, 1867.

MY DEAR LORD BISHOP,

Understanding that there has been some misapprehension on the part of the American bishops as to their invitation to a service in Westminster Abbey, I beg that you will do me the favour of communicating the following statement, in as public a way as you may think fit, to your Episcopal brethren.

It was impossible for me, as guardian of a building like the Abbey, which belongs to the whole Church and people of England, to take the responsibility of giving its sanction to a meeting which included only a portion of the English bishops, and of which the objects were undefined, the issues unknown, and the discussions secret. But I was so anxious to show every courtesy to the bishops from the United States, that, chiefly on their own account, as I particularly specified in my letter to the Archbishop of Canterbury, I so far deviated from the usual rules which guide the services in the Abbey as to propose the use of the Abbey for a service which should gather them there, either for some specific object of usefulness or charity or for the general promotion of goodwill and edification amongst all members of the Anglican Communion. I was encouraged the more to make this offer by the pledge that I had received that no questions exciting party differences should be introduced into the meetings, and I was therefore in hopes that his Grace would have felt himself able to accept a proposal which I had reason to believe would be gratifying to our American brethren.

The proposal was, however, declined ; and I must therefore, through you, beg to express my regret that such an opportunity was lost of cultivating those feelings of amity between the two countries which are at all times so welcome.

The circumstances of the severe domestic affliction which has recently befallen us, whilst they prevented me from showing that hospitality which I should otherwise have offered to you, make me doubly anxious that, in a country from which we have received expressions of such sincere sympathy, there should be no misunderstanding as to the cordial desire that I entertain to welcome Americans on all occasions to our joint national sanctuary.

I trust that on some future occasion I may take the opportunity of renewing personally my assurance of the pleasure which it will ever give me to receive the citizens of a nation in which we must always feel peculiar interest.

I beg to remain,
Yours faithfully,
A. P. STANLEY.

No. X. (See page 15.)

REPORTS OF COMMITTEES APPOINTED BY THE CONFERENCE OF 1867.

A.—*Report of the Committee appointed under Resolution V., by the Conference of Bishops of the Anglican Communion, held at Lambeth Palace, September 24-27th, 1867.*

The subject of the functions and relations of the several Synods, on which the Committee is appointed to report, appears to them to be necessarily connected with questions as to the constitution of these bodies. The following Report, therefore, embraces the whole subject of Synods. In discussing it, your Committee deems it necessary to deal with the question in the abstract, without reference to existing laws and usages in the several branches of the Anglican Communion, and to lay down general principles, the adoption or application of which must depend on circumstances, such, for example, as the laws which any Church may have inherited or already established.

---

[1] Resolution IV.—" That, in the opinion of this Conference, Unity in Faith and Discipline will be best maintained among the several branches of the Anglican Communion by due and canonical subordination of the Synods of the several branches to the higher authority of a Synod or Synods above them."

Resolution V.—" That a Committee of seven members (with power to add to their number, and to obtain the assistance of men learned in Ecclesiastical and Canon Law) be appointed to inquire into and report upon the subject of the relations and functions of such Synods, and that such Report be forwarded to his Grace the Lord Archbishop of Canterbury, with a request that, if possible, it may be communicated to any adjourned meeting of this Conference."

I.—In the organisation of Synodal order for the government of the Church, the Diocesan Synod appears to be the primary and simplest form of such organisation.

By the Diocesan Synod the co-operation of all members of the body is obtained in Church action ; and that acceptance of Church rules is secured, which, in the absence of other law, usage, or enactment, gives to these rules the force of laws " binding on those who, expressly or by implication, have consented to them.[1]"

For this reason, wherever the Church is not established by law, it is, in the judgment of your Committee, essential to order and good government that the Diocese should be organised by a Synod.

Your Committee consider that it is not at variance with the ancient principles of the Church, that both Clergy and Laity should attend the Diocesan Synod, and that it is expedient that the Synod should consist of the Bishop and Clergy of the Diocese, with Representives of the Laity.

The constitution of the Diocesan Synod may be determined either by rules for that branch of the Church established by the Synod of the Province, or by general consent in the Diocese itself, its rules being sanctioned afterwards by the Provincial Synod.

Your Committee, however, recommend that the following general rules should be adopted ; viz., that the Bishop, Clergy, and Laity should sit together, the Bishop presiding ; that votes should be taken by orders, whenever demanded ; and that the concurrent assent of Bishop, Clergy, and Laity should be necessary to the validity of all acts of the Synod.

They consider that the Clerical members of the Synod should be those Clergy who are recognized by the Bishop, according to the rules of the Church

---

[1] Judgment of Judicial Committee of Privy Council in case of Long *v.* Bishop of Capetown. 1 Moore, P. C. C., N.S., 461.

in that Diocese, as being under his jurisdiction. Whether in large Dioceses, when the Clergy are very numerous, they might appear by representation, is a difficult question, and one on which your Committee are not prepared to express an opinion.

The Lay Representatives in the Synod ought, in the judgment of your Committee, to be Male Communicants of at least one year's standing in the Diocese, and of the full age of twenty-one. It should be required that the electors should be Members of the Church in that Diocese, and belong to the parish in which they claim to vote. It appears desirable that the regular meetings of the Synod should be fixed and periodical; but that the right of convening special meetings whenever they may be required should be reserved to the Bishop.

The office of the Diocesan Synod is, generally, to make regulations, not repugnant to those of higher Synods, for the order and good government of the Church within the Diocese, and to promulgate the decisions of the Provincial Synod.

II.—The Provincial Synod—or, as it is called in New Zealand, the General Synod, and in the United States the General Convention—is formed, whenever it does not exist already by law and usage, through the voluntary association of Dioceses for united legislation and common action. The Provincial Synod not only provides a method for securing unity amongst the Dioceses which are thus associated, but also forms the link between these Dioceses and other Churches of the Anglican Communion.

Without questioning the right of the Bishops of any Province to meet in Synod by themselves, and without affirming that the presence of others is essential to a Provincial Synod, your Committee recommend that, whenever no law or usage to the contrary already exists, it should consist of the Bishops of the Province, and of Representatives both of the Clergy and of the Laity in each Diocese.

Your Committee need not define the method in which a Provincial Synod may be first constituted, but they assume that its constitution and rules will be determined by the concurrence of the several Dioceses duly represented.

Your Committee consider that it must be left to each Province to decide whether, and under what circumstances, the Bishops, Clergy, and Laity in a Provincial Synod should sit and discuss questions in the same chamber or separately; but, in the judgment of the Committee, the votes should in either case be taken by orders; and the concurrent assent of Bishops, Clergy, and Laity should be necessary for any legislative action, wherever the Clergy and Laity form part of the constitution of a Provincial Synod; such powers and functions not involving legislation being reserved as belong to the Bishops by virtue of their office.

The number, qualification, and mode of election of the Clerical and Lay Representatives from each Diocese must be determined by the Synods in the several Provinces.

It is the office of the Provincial Synod, generally, to exercise, within the limits of the Province, powers in regard to Provincial questions similar to those which the Diocesan Synod exercises, within the Diocese, in regard to Diocesan questions.

As to the relation between these two Synods, your Committee are of opinion that the Diocese is bound to accept positive enactments of a Provincial Synod in which it is duly represented, and that no Diocesan regulations have force, if contrary to the decisions of a higher Synod; but that, in order to prevent any collision or misunderstanding, the spheres of action of the several Synods should be defined on the following principle, viz., That the Provincial Synod should deal with questions of common interest to the whole Province, and with those which affect the communion of the Dioceses with one another and with the rest of the Church; whilst the Diocesan Synod should be left free to dispose of matters of local interest, and to manage the affairs of the Diocese.

From this principle your Committee draws the following conclusions :—

1. All alterations in the Services of the Church, required by circumstances in the Province, should be made or authorized by the Provincial Synod, and not merely by the Diocesan.

2. The rule of discipline for the Clergy of the Province should be framed by the Provincial Synod.

3. Rules for the trial of Clergy should be made by the Provincial Synod; but, in default of such action on the part of that Synod, the Diocesan Synod should establish provisional rules for this purpose. The Provincial Tribunal of Appeal should be established by the Provincial Synod.

4. In questions relating to Patronage, the tenure of Church property, Parochial divisions, arrangements, officers, &c., there should be joint action of the Diocese and the Province; the former making such regulations as may be best suited to develop local resources, the latter providing against the admission of any principle inexpedient for the common interests of the Church.

5. The erection of a new Diocese within the limits of an existing Diocese should proceed by general rules established by the Provincial Synod.

6. The question of the election of a Bishop it is unnecessary here to consider, as it is submitted to another Committee.

III.—The question of a higher Synod of the Anglican Communion, and of the relation which the inferior Synods should hold towards it, whenever it might assemble, is one, your Committee are aware, of much greater difficulty than any of those which have been previously considered.

The fact, however, that a Conference of Bishops of the whole Anglican Communion has already met together, is of itself an indication of the need which is generally felt of united counsel in a sphere more extensive than that of a Provincial Synod. Indeed, the Resolutions under which this Committee was appointed contemplate the possibility at least of some Synod being established superior to the Provincial. It is also implied in Resolution VIII. of this Conference, that some such Assembly may be required, in order to preserve Colonial and Missionary Churches in close union with the Church of England, since it is provided that all changes in the Services of the Church made by one of their Provincial Synods should " be liable to revision by any Synod of the Anglican Communion in which the said Province should be represented."

The objections that may be urged against the united action of Churches which are more or less free to act independently, and other Churches whose constitution is fixed, not only by ancient ecclesiastical laws and usages, but by the law of the State, are obvious; but it appears to your Committee that the action of this Conference has proved that the difficulties which are anticipated are not insuperable, and suggests the method by which they may be overcome. Under present circumstances, indeed, no Assembly that might be convened would be competent to enact canons of binding ecclesiastical authority on these different bodies, or to frame definitions of faith which it would be obligatory on the Churches of the Anglican Communion to accept. It would be necessary, therefore, in the judgment of your Committee, to avoid all terms respecting this Assembly that might imply authority of this nature, and to call it a Congress, if even the term Council should be considered open to objection. Its decisions could only possess the authority which might be derived from the moral weight of such united counsels and judgments, and from the voluntary acceptance of its conclusions by any of the Churches there represented.

Your Committee consider that his Grace the Archbishop of Canterbury, as occupying the See from which the Colonial and American Churches derive their succession, should be the convener of such an Assembly. That it should differ from the present Conference in being attended by both Clerical and Lay Representatives of the several Churches, as consultees and advisers, each Diocese being allowed to send, besides its Bishop, a presbyter and a lay member of the Church, if they should desire to be thus represented; and further, in the proceedings being more formal and, in part at least, public. The question when for the first time, and at what periods, this Congress or Council should be called, your Committee deem it more respectful to leave for the consideration of his Grace the Archbishop of Canterbury and of the present Conference.

                        G. A. NEW ZEALAND, *Chairman*.
                        H. GRAHAMSTOWN, *Secretary*.

B.—*Report of the Committee appointed under Resolution IX. of the Lambeth Conference, on the Constitution of a voluntary spiritual Tribunal, to which questions of Doctrine may be carried by Appeal from the Tribunals for the exercise of discipline in each Province of the Colonial Church.*[1]

After full consideration of objections that have been urged against the establishment of any such Tribunal as that contemplated by this Resolution, your Committee are of opinion that these objections are not sufficient to outweigh the arguments in its favour, and that most of the objections will be found inapplicable to the particular form of Tribunal which the Committee recommend.

Your Committee consider that such a Tribunal is required in order to prevent the dissatisfaction which would arise if important questions were finally decided by those Colonial Churches, the circumstances of which render it impossible for them to form a sufficient Tribunal of last resort.

It would also tend to secure unity in matters of Faith, and uniformity in matters of Discipline, where Doctrine may be involved.

For these reasons your Committee recommend that such a Tribunal be established ; and, from the desire

---

[1] Resolution IX.—"That the Committee appointed by Resolution V., with the addition of the names of the Bishops of London, St. David's, and Oxford, and all the Colonial Bishops, be instructed to consider the constitution of a voluntary spiritual Tribunal, to which questions of doctrine may be carried by appeal from the Tribunals for the exercise of discipline in each Province of the Colonial Church, and that their report be forwarded to his Grace the Lord Archbishop of Canterbury, who is requested to communicate it to an adjourned meeting of this Conference."

expressed by several branches of the Colonial Church, that this should be one of the results of this Conference, they believe that it will be generally accepted by those for whose benefit it is designed.

At the same time, they are sensible of the great difficulty of forming such a Tribunal, and of the necessity of proceeding with caution, lest it should interfere with the liberties of the Colonial Churches, or should have any appearance of collision with the Courts established by law, either here or in Her Majesty's foreign possessions.

Your Committee now proceed to lay before the Conference their conclusions as to the functions and constitution of the proposed Tribunal.

They are of opinion that it should not take cognizance of any case which shall not have been referred to it by some branch of the Anglican Communion which has consented to its constitution. Thus it would not interfere either with those Churches in which provision is made by the State for the exercise of discipline, or with the liberty and rights of ecclesiastical Provinces. These would be free to accept or to decline the appeal thus offered to them, and to withdraw afterwards their acceptance of the Tribunal, if they should so desire.[1]

Your Committee consider that this Tribunal of Appeal should take into consideration all the facts of the case as sent up to it in writing from the inferior Tribunal; that the Appeal, however, should not be on the facts, but only on the points of Doctrine and Discipline involved in them.

That during the Appeal the sentence of the Provincial Tribunal should continue in force, so far as it

---

[1] The decisions of such a Tribunal would be of the same nature as those of "arbitrators, whose jurisdiction rests entirely upon the agreement of the parties." (Judgment of Judicial Committee of the Privy Council in case of Long *v.* Bishop of Capetown, 1 Moore, P. C. C., N.S. 462.)

affects the present exercise of spiritual functions by the accused.

That the judgments of the Tribunal of Appeal should be delivered in the form of a decision that the teaching or practice of the accused party is (or is not) permissible.

That the Tribunal should use as the standards of faith and doctrine by which its decisions shall be governed, those which are now in use in the United Church of England and Ireland; and that as to all matters not defined in such formularies, the judgments should be framed on any conclusions which shall be hereafter agreed to at any Council or Congress of the whole Anglican Communion: Provided always, that no such conclusion be contradictory to any now existing standard or formulary of the Church of England; and provided further, that the Synod of that Province of the Church from which the Appeal shall be sent, shall not have refused to accept such conclusion.

Your Committee further recommend, subject to any regulations that may be made at any future Conference of the Anglican Communion :—

That, as it is a Tribunal for decisions in matters of faith, Archbishops and Bishops only should be judges, his Grace the Lord Archbishop of Canterbury being the President.

That each Province in the Colonial Church should have the right of electing two members of the Tribunal; and that all the Dioceses of the Colonial Church not associated into Provinces should collectively have the right of electing two. That each Province of the United Church of England and Ireland should be requested to elect two members, but that the Province of Canterbury should elect three, in the event of his Grace the Archbishop not acting as President. That the Episcopal Church in Scotland should have the right of electing two. And (as it appears probable that the Protestant Episcopal

Church in the United States would avail itself of such a Tribunal) that Church should have the right of electing five members.

In the judgment of the Committee, the Bishops of the several Churches should elect those who shall represent them on this Tribunal.

That, so soon after January 1, 1869, as any ten names shall have been forwarded to the Archbishop of Canterbury as having been elected, the Tribunal should be deemed to be constituted.

That of the members thus elected, seven should form a quorum for the transaction of business, but a smaller number should have power to adjourn from time to time.

That the members of the Tribunal should continue in office, unless their seat be vacated by death, resignation, or removal by the electing body; but that, in the event of any Bishop of the Colonial or American Church notifying to the electing body that he is unable or declines to attend at any sitting of the Tribunal to which he may be summoned, it should be lawful for the body by which he was elected to appoint, instead of him, any Bishop of the Anglican Communion other than one of those already elected.

That, in the event of the Archbishop of Canterbury for the time being declining or being unable to act as President, it should be lawful for his Grace, if he should see fit, to nominate any other member of the Tribunal to act as President in his room; and in the event of no such appointment being made by him, that it should be lawful for the Tribunal at its first meeting to elect one of its members as President.

That the summons for the sitting of the Tribunal should be issued within thirty days from the time of the notice of Appeal being delivered by the agent of the Appellant to the proper officer of the Tribunal.

That the action of the Tribunal should not be

impeded by the absence from it of any of those who are at liberty to sit in it, provided there be a quorum.

That, before the assembling of the Tribunal for the hearing of an Appeal, the President should nominate as Assessors three theologians and three persons learned in the law, who should be present at the trial, and should answer any questions as to theological learning and law put to them by the Tribunal through its President in writing, and who should be at liberty to tender in writing to the Tribunal through its President their opinion upon any point of theological learning or law which may arise, and that the Tribunal should be bound to consider such opinion before coming to its decision.

That parties before the Tribunal may be represented by any counsel they may select, whether theologians or persons learned in the law.

That the rules of procedure of the said Tribunal, except as here provided for, should, as far as possible, be those of the higher Courts of Law, and that any necessary alterations in such rules should be made by the Tribunal itself.

That no sentence should be passed without the assent thereto of two-thirds of the Judges present during the trial.

That, at the time of delivering judgment, each member of the Tribunal who has been present during the trial should give his decision in writing, and may read, or cause to be read, openly in Court his decision, and the reasons for it; and that the judgment of the prescribed majority should be the judgment of the Tribunal.

     F. MONTREAL, *Chairman.*
     H. GRAHAMSTOWN, *Secretary.*

C.—*On the Courts of Metropolitans, and the Trial of a Bishop or Metropolitan.*[1]

I. Your Committee consider that the constitution of the Provincial Tribunal for Appeals from the decisions of Diocesan Tribunals should be determined, whenever it is not fixed by law, by the Synod of the Province; but it is expedient, in their judgment, that its rules should be assimilated, as far as circumstances will admit, to those of the proposed tribunal of Appeal in England.

II. In the case of charges against a Bishop, they suggest the following as general principles:—

That each Province should determine by rules made in its own Synod the offences for which a Bishop may be presented for trial, and who should be promoters of the charge.

That the charge should be presented to the Metropolitan.

That it appears doubtful whether a preliminary inquiry is expedient, provided that sufficient precautions are taken that no frivolous charges should be entertained.

That the Metropolitan should summon to the hearing of the cause all the Bishops of the Province (except the accused), who should sit as judges, not merely as assessors.

---

[1] Resolution X.—"That the Resolutions submitted to this Conference relative to the discipline to be exercised by the Metropolitans, the Court of Metropolitans, the scheme for conducting the Election of Bishops, when not otherwise provided for, the declaration of submission to the Regulation of Synods, and the question of what Legislation should be proposed for the Colonial Churches, be referred to the Committee specified in the preceding Resolution."

That no trial should take place, except before two-thirds of the Bishops of the Province, provided that there be never fewer than three Bishops present, including the Metropolitan.

That if three Bishops of the Province should be unable to attend, it should be lawful for the Metropolitan to call in one or more Bishops not of the Province.

That it is desirable that, whenever it may be practicable, there should be Assessors, as recommended by this Committee for the higher Tribunal of Appeal.

That, in case of the non-appearance of the accused after sufficient citations, the trial may go forward as if he were present, or he may be punished for contumacy, according as the Province may prescribe.

That there should be no sentence except by the judgment of two-thirds of the Tribunal, or by three judges, whichever should be the greater number; the assent of the Metropolitan not being necessary to the sentence.

That the general rules of procedure should be framed by the Synod of the Province; but should be, as far as possible, similar to those recommended by this Committee for the proposed Tribunal of Appeal.

That an appeal to the higher Tribunal recommended by this Committee should be allowed when the case is one of doctrine, or discipline involving doctrine, if notice of such appeal be given within   days from the delivery of sentence; and that, in all cases, proper provision should be made for a new trial on sufficient reason being shown.

That there should be no contract not to appeal to Civil Courts; but that sufficient provision should be made by the Declaration of Submission (to be considered in another Report) that the sentence of the Spiritual Tribunals may be effective.

That a Metropolitan should be tried in the same manner as any other Bishop—the senior Bishop, in that case, acting in the place of the Metropolitan.

F. MONTREAL, *Chairman.*
H. GRAHAMSTOWN, *Secretary.*

D.—*Scheme for conducting the Election of Bishops, when not otherwise provided for.*

Your Committee have to consider the proper mode for conducting the election of a Bishop, whenever it is not provided for by an existing law, and without reference to any question that might arise as to the temporalities connected with the See.

It is evident that there are two parties whose concurrent action is necessary in such an appointment —viz., the Clergy and Laity of the Diocese, and the Bishops of the Province by whom the person elected as Bishop is consecrated.

Your Committee are of opinion that, in accordance with the ancient usages of the Church, the election as a general rule should be made by the Diocese, and that the Bishops of the Province should confirm the election. They consider, however, that it is consistent with this principle that the Diocese should nominate two or more persons, of whom the Bishops of the Province should select one; or that the Diocese should delegate to any person or body the power of choosing a Bishop for the vacant See, it being understood that the Diocese must accept such choice as final.

The principle of the concurrent action of the two parties concerned would also be preserved if the Bishops of the Province should nominate two or more persons, from whom the Diocese should elect one.

In the election by the Diocese it appears to your Committee that the right of selecting the person who shall be their Bishop belongs to the Clergy, the Laity having the right of accepting or rejecting the person so chosen. But it is expedient, in their judgment, that the election should always be made by the Diocesan Synod, wherever one is established, and in accordance with the rules of that Synod. In those Dioceses in which there is no Diocesan Synod, they recommend that, for the election of a Bishop, a Convention should be summoned by the Dean, senior Archdeacon, or senior Presbyter of the Diocese; that this Convention should consist of all Presbyters and of lay-representatives, who should be male communicants of at least twenty-one years of age; that these representatives should be elected by each parish or congregation, in such manner as should be determined by the convener; that the person who should obtain the majority of votes of the Clergy, and also of those of the lay-representatives present at the Convention, should be accounted to be elected to the Bishopric; that this election should not be vitiated by the absence of any of the parties summoned, or by the failure of any congregation or parish to elect a lay-representative; that any question as to the validity of the election to the vacant See should be submitted, prior to the Consecration, to the Consecrating Bishops, whose decision should be final; and that after the consecration of a Bishop no objection should be entertained.

They further recommend that, where the Diocese is included in a Province, the confirmation of an election should be by the Metropolitan and a majority of the Bishops of the Province; but where the Diocese is extra-Provincial, that the confirmation should rest with the Archbishops of Canterbury and York and the Bishop of London; that the power of confirmation should be absolute—the Bishops having the right to refuse to confirm the election, without assigning any reason for their refusal.

All further rules necessary for conducting the election should, in the opinion of your Committee, be made by the Synod of the Province.

F. MONTREAL, *Chairman.*
H. GRAHAMSTOWN, *Secretary.*

E.—*On Declaration of Submission to Regulations of Synod.*

Your Committee recommend that, in all branches of the Church, the government of which is not determined by law, a Declaration should be made by those who hold office therein. They consider that a Declaration is necessary, in order to define the conditions of the consensual compact, and that it should be framed so as to secure submission to all synodical action in its legitimate sphere, and to the decisions of the constituted Tribunals.

They recommend the following declaration to be made, before the Metropolitan, or some person duly appointed by him, by all Bishops elect, either before their consecration or, if already consecrated, before exercising any Episcopal functions in their diocese :—

"I *A. B.*, chosen Bishop of the Church and See of   , do promise that I will teach and maintain the doctrine and discipline of the United Church of England and Ireland, as acknowledged and received by the Province of   , and I also do declare that I consent to be bound by all the rules and regulations which have heretofore been made or which may from time to time be made, by the Synod of the Diocese of   , and the Provincial Synod of   , or either of them; and, in consideration of being appointed Bishop of the said Church or See of   , I hereby undertake immediately to resign the said appointment, together with all the rights and emoluments appertaining thereto, if sentence requiring such resignation should at any time be passed upon me, after due examination had, by the Tribunal acknowledged by the Synod of the said Province for the trial of a Bishop ;. saving all rights of Appeal allowed by the said Synod."

They recommend that the following Declaration be made (in addition to the Declaration required by the rules of that Province or Diocese as to doctrine and worship) by persons to be admitted to holy orders, and by Clergymen to be admitted to the cure of souls, or to any other office of trust in the Church.

" I, *A. B.*, do declare that I consent to be bound by all the rules and regulations which have heretofore been made, or which may from time to time be made, by the Synod of the Diocese of   , and the Provincial Synod of   , or either of them ; [and in consideration of being appointed   , I hereby undertake immediately to resign the said appointment, together with all the rights and emoluments appertaining thereto, if sentence requiring such resignation should at any time be passed upon me, after due examination had, by the Tribunal appointed by the Synods of the aforesaid Province and Diocese for the trial of a Clergyman ; saving all rights of Appeal allowed by the said Synod]."

(The part in brackets to be omitted when there is no appointment to a cure of souls, or office of trust).

Your Committee consider that it must be left to the Province or Diocese to decide whether laymen who are admitted to any office or position of trust should be required to sign a Declaration of the same nature.

G. A. NEW ZEALAND,
Chairman.

H. GRAHAMSTOWN,
Secretary.

F.—*On Provinces and Subordination to Metropolitans.*

On this subject your Committee beg to report as follows :—

They are of opinion that the association or federation of Dioceses within certain territorial limits, commonly called an Ecclesiastical Province, is not only in accordance with the ancient laws and usages of the Christian Church, but is essential to its complete organization.

Such an association is of the highest advantage for united action, for the exercise of discipline, for the confirmation of the election of Bishops, and generally to enable the Church to adapt its laws to the circumstances of the countries in which it is planted.

It is expedient, in the judgment of your Committee, that these ecclesiastical divisions should, as far as possible, follow the civil divisions of these countries.

Of the Bishops of these Dioceses thus associated, one, in conformity with ancient usage, ought to be Metropolitan or Primus, the functions and powers of the Metropolitan being determined by synodical action in the Province, except so far as Metropolitical powers are defined by undisputed General Councils of the Church.

It seems to your Committee most in accordance

with primitive usage that the Metropolitical see should be fixed, but they do not deem this to be essential. It appears expedient that the Provincial Synod should have the power of changing, when necessary, the site of the Metropolitical see.

Your Committee do not consider it necessary that the election to the Metropolitical see should be conducted differently from the election to other vacant sees; since the Bishops of the Province possess the right of confirming or refusing to confirm any election.

Your Committee strongly recommend that all those Dioceses which are not as yet gathered into Provinces should, as soon as possible, form part of some Provincial organization. The particular mode of effecting this in each case must be determined by those who are concerned.

It is sufficient for your Committee to point out that the steps to be taken for effecting this change are two-fold, since the relations of the Dioceses in Provincial organisation, when complete, are formed on the one hand by the subordination of the Bishops of the Province to a Metropolitan, and on the other by the association of the Dioceses in Provincial action. Any alteration of existing arrangements would require, therefore, in the opinion of your Committee, the concurrent action of the Diocese which is to be gathered into a Province with other neighbouring Dioceses, and of his Grace the Archbishop of Canterbury, to whom the Bishops of the Dioceses that at present are extra-provincial have taken the oath of canonical obedience. In the case of the limits of an existing Province being altered, the consent of the Synod of that Province would be required for the alteration.

F. MONTREAL, *Chairman.*
H. GRAHAMSTOWN, *Secretary.*

G.—*Report of the Committee appointed under Resolution XI. of the Lambeth Conference.*[1]

Your Committee report that, after full consideration of the questions referred to them by the Conference, they have adopted the following Resolutions :—

I. That every branch of the Church is entitled to found a Missionary Bishopric.

II. That it is desirable that each branch of the Church should act upon rules agreed upon beforehand by the Synod or other Church Council of the said branch.

III. That each Missionary Bishopric should be deemed to be attached to one branch of the Church, and that all rules for the election of a Missionary Bishop, and for the formation of a Diocese or Dioceses out of the Missionary District, should be made by the Synod or other Church Council of such branch of the Church.

IV. That notice of the erection of any Missionary Bishopric, and the choice and consecration of the Bishop, should be notified to all Archbishops and Metropolitans, and all Presiding Bishops, of the Anglican Communion.

V. That in appointing a Missionary Bishop, the district within which he is to exercise his Mission should be defined as far as possible; and that no other Bishop should be sent within the same district,

---

[1] Resolution XI.—"That a Special Committee be appointed to consider the Resolutions relative to the Notification of proposed Missionary Bishoprics, and the Subordination of Missionaries."

without previous communication with that branch of the Church which gave mission for the work.

VI. That, while peculiar cases may occur in Missionary work, owing to difference of race and language, in which it may be desirable that more than one Bishop should exercise episcopal functions within the same district, the Committee consider that such cases should be regarded as exceptions, justified only by special circumstances.

VII. That, with respect to the special case of Continental Chaplaincies, the Committee suggest to the Conference the consideration of some ecclesiastical arrangement by which the various congregations of the Anglican Communion may be under one authority, whether of the English or American Church.

VIII. That the conditions on which a Missionary Bishopric should be brought within a Provincial organisation should be:—

1. The request of the Missionary Bishop, addressed both to the Church from which he received mission and to the Province which he wishes to join.

2. The consent of the Church from which he received mission, that consent being given by the Metropolitan or Presiding Bishop.

3. The consent of the Province he wishes to join, that consent being given by the Provincial Synod.

IX. That the status, jurisdiction, and designation of the Bishop thus received into a system of Provincial organisation should be determined by the Synod of the Province to which his Bishopric shall be then attached.

X. That, as a general rule, it is expedient that such Missionary Bishopric should be attached to the nearest Province; but that in certain cases it may be necessary that some more remote Province should be selected.

Bishop Tozer's Mission is a case to which the

Committee desire to draw the attention of the Conference, as being one in which, for the present, Provincial organization would seem to be impracticable, from the isolation of the district in which Bishop Tozer exercises his episcopal functions, and its remoteness from the Province of South Africa.

XI. That Missionary Bishops and their Clergy should be bound generally to the Canons of Doctrine and Discipline of the Church from which their mission is derived, or to which they may have been united, and that all alterations in matters of discipline be communicated to the authorities of that Church.

XII. That when a Missionary Church shall be received into the organisation of a Provincial Synod, the said Church should be bound by the acts of that body; but that, in order to effect this, the Missionary Church should be granted a power of representation, or of vote by proxy, in such Synod.

XIII. That, as a general rule, in conformity with Church order, all Missionaries and Chaplains residing or engaged in the exercise of ministerial duty within the Diocese or District of a Colonial or Missionary Bishop, should be licensed by, and be subject to the authority of, the said Bishop.

XIV. That every Clergyman removing from one Colonial or Missionary Diocese or District into another Diocese ought to carry with him Letters Testimonial from the Colonial or Missionary Bishop whose Diocese or District he is leaving.

XV. That no person admitted to Holy Orders by the Bishop of any Diocese in England or Ireland, who shall afterwards have been serving under the jurisdiction of any Scottish, Colonial, or Foreign Bishop, should be received into any of the Home Dioceses, without producing letters Dimissory or Commendatory from the Scottish, Colonial, or Foreign Bishop in whose Diocese he has been serving.

XVI. The attention of this Committee has been

called to the clause in the Paper of Arrangements for the Conference, headed "Subordination of Missionaries." The Committee have failed to understand what is meant by the words "instructions from those in authority at home," but they can recommend no scheme which interferes with the canonical relation which subsists between a Bishop and his clery.

W. J. GIBRALTAR,
Chairman.

WILLIAM GEORGE TOZER,.
MISSIONARY BISHOP,
Secretary.

H.—Report of the Committee appointed under Resolution VI. of the Lambeth Conference.[1]

By the Resolution of the Lambeth Conference two questions were referred to the Committee :—

I. How the Church may be delivered from a continuance of the scandal now existing in Natal?

II. How the true faith may be maintained?

I. On the first question, the Committee recommend that an Address be made to the Colonial

---

[1] Resolution VI.—"That, in the judgment of the Bishops now assembled, the whole Anglican Communion is deeply injured by the present condition of the Church in Natal : and that a Committee be now appointed at this General Meeting to report on the best mode by which the Church may be delivered from a continuance of this scandal, and the true faith maintained. That such Report shall be forwarded to his Grace the Lord Archbishop of Canterbury, with the request that he will be pleased to transmit the same to all the Bishops of the Anglican Communion, and to ask for their judgment thereupon."

Bishoprics Council, calling their attention to the fact that they are paying an annual stipend to a Bishop lying under the imputation of heretical teaching, and praying them to take the best legal opinion as to there being any, and if so what, mode mode of laying these allegations before some competent court, and if any mode be pointed out, then to proceed accordingly for the removal of this scandal.

The Committee also recommend that the Address to the Colonial Bishoprics Council be prefaced with the following statement:—

"That, whilst we accept the spiritual validity of the sentence of deposition pronounced by the Metropolitan and Bishops of the South African Church upon Dr. Colenso, we consider it of the utmost moment for removing the existing scandal from the English Communion that there should be pronounced by some competent English court such a legal sentence on the errors of the said Dr. Colenso as would warrant the Colonial Bishoprics Council in ceasing to pay his stipend, and would justify an appeal to the Crown to cancel his Letters Patent."

II. On the second question:

"How the true faith may be maintained in Natal?"

The Committee submit the following Report:—

That they did not consider themselves instructed by the Conference, and therefore did not consider themselves competent, to inquire into the whole case; but that their conclusions are based upon the following facts:—

1. That in the year 1863, *forty-one* Bishops concurred in an Address to Bishop Colenso, urging him to resign his Bishopric.

2. That in the year 1863, some of the publications of Dr. Colenso, viz.—"The Pentateuch and Book of Joshua critically examined," Parts I. and II., were condemned by the Convocation of the Province of Canterbury."

3. That the Bishop of Capetown, by virtue of his

Letters Patent as Metropolitan, might have visited Dr. Colenso with summary jurisdiction, and might have taken out of his hands the management of the Diocese of Natal.

4. That the Bishop of Capetown, instead of proceeding summarily, instituted judicial proceedings, having reason to believe himself to be competent to do so.

That he summoned Dr. Colenso before himself and suffragans.

That Dr. Colenso appeared by his proctor.

That his defence was heard and judged to be insufficient to purge him from the heresy.

That, after sentence was pronounced, Dr. Colenso was offered an appeal to the Archbishop of Canterbury, as provided in the Metropolitan's Letters Patent.

5. That this Act of the African Church was approved—

By the Convocation of Canterbury;

By the Convocation of York;

By the General Convention of the Episcopal Church in the United States, in 1865;

By the Episcopal Synod of the Church in Scotland;

By the Provincial Synod of the Church in Canada, in the year 1865;

And, finally, the spiritual validity of the sentence of deposition was accepted by *fifty-six* Bishops on the occasion of the Lambeth Conference.

Judging, therefore, that the See is spiritually vacant; and learning, by the evidence brought before them, that there are many members of the Church who are unable to accept the ministrations of Dr. Colenso, the Committee deem it to be the duty of the Metropolitan and other Bishops of South Africa to proceed, upon the election of the Clergy and Laity in Natal, to consecate one to discharge those spiritual functions of which these members of the Church are now in want.

In forwarding their Report to his Grace the Lord Archbishop of Canterbury, as instructed by the Resolution of the Conference, the Committee request his Grace to communicate the same to the adjourned meeting of the Conference, to be holden at Lambeth on the tenth day of the present month.

G. A. NEW ZEALAND,

December 9th, 1867. *Convener.*

J.—*Form of Letters Dimissory for the Clergy.*

To the Right Reverend the Bishops and Reverend the Clergy, and to the faithful in Christ of the Diocese of A. We, B, by Divine permission Bishops of C, send greeting in the Lord.

We commend to your brotherly kindness by these our letters, D, E, Priest (or Deacon) of our Diocese, beseeching you to receive him in the Lord as a brother sound in the Faith, of a well-ordered and Religious Life, and worthy of all Christian Fellowship, and to render him any assistance of which he may stand in need; and so we bid you farewell in Christ our Lord.

Witness our hand.

A, Bishop.
B, Secretary.

No. XI. (See page 15.)

Resolutions of the Adjourned Conference, Dec. 10, 1867.

Resolution I.—" That this adjourned meeting of the Conference receives the Report (No. I.) of the Committee now presented, and directs the publication thereof, commending it to the careful consideration of the Bishops of the Anglican Communion, as containing the result of the deliberations of that Committee; and returns the members of the same its thanks for the care with which they have considered the various important questions referred to them."

(The same Resolution was passed with reference to Reports II., III., IV., V., VI., VII.)

Resolution II.—" That the Report (No. VIII.) of the Committee appointed under Resolution VI., laid before this meeting by his Grace the Archbishop of Canterbury be received and printed; that the thanks of this Meeting be given to the Committee for their labours; and that his Grace be requested to communicate the Report to the Council of the Colonial Bishoprics Fund."

Resolution III.—" That his Grace be requested, if applied to by the House of Bishops in the Episcopal Church in the United States of America, to allow a copy of the Records of the Conference to be made for them, and to be lodged in the hands of such officer as shall be designated by the House of Bishops to receive it, for reference by Bishops only, but not for publication."

Resolution IV.—" That his Grace the Archbishop of Canterbury be requested to convey to the Church in Russia an expression of the sympathy of the Anglican Communion with that Church, in the loss which it has sustained by the death of his Eminence Philarete, the venerable Metropolitan of Moscow."

Resolution V.—" That the thanks of this Conference be given to the Bishop of Grahamstown for the valuable services which he has rendered as Secretary to many of the Committees appointed by the Conference."

Resolution VI.—" That the thanks of this Conference be given to Philip Wright, Esq., and to Isambard Brunel, Esq., Barrister-at-Law, for their aid as

Assistant Secretaries to the Committees; and especially to the latter for his valuable assistance in all matters that required legal advice."

Resolution VII.—" That we cannot close this Conference without conveying our hearty thanks to his Grace the Archbishop of Canterbury, both for convening this meeting, and for the mode in which he has presided over its deliberations."

Besides the preceding Resolutions,—

The President reported that he had been authorised to annex the following signatures to the Encyclical Letter :—

>A. T. CICESTR.
>AUCKLAND, BATH AND WELLS.
>ROBERT DOWN AND CONNOR.
>WILLIAM DERRY.
>EDWARD NEWFOUNDLAND.
>J. FREDERICTON.
>T. E. ST. HELENA.

2. The following Bishops were appointed as a Sub-Committee, for the purpose of drawing up a Bill, in accordance with a Report submitted by the Committee appointed under Resolution IX. of the previous meeting :—

>BISHOP OF LONDON.
>   "   OXFORD.
>   "   LINCOLN.
>   "   ELY.
>   "   LICHFIELD (Elect).
>   "   MONTREAL.
>   "   GRAHAMSTOWN.
>BISHOP TROWER.

3. His Grace the Archbishop of Canterbury laid on the table a form of Letters Dimissory,[1] which he had prepared, in accordance with Resolution II. of the last session of the Lambeth Conference.

---

[1] J. page 98.

4. The Bishop of Illinois, at the request of the Conference, stated that the Meeting of the Triennial General Convention of the Protestant Episcopal Church in the United States would be held on the first Wednesday of October next, in the City of New York; and, in behalf of the Church in the United States, offered an affectionate invitation to the Bishops of the Conference to be present on that occasion; and also expressed the hope that the different branches of the Anglican Communion would depute one or more Bishops as Representatives of the Mother and Colonial Churches, to be present on that occasion, assuring all that might accept this invitation of cordial welcome and affectionate brotherhood.

5. At the request of the Conference, the Bishop of Lichfield (Elect) undertook the office of Corresponding Secretary for the Bishops of the Anglican Communion.

His Grace the President then pronounced the Benediction, and the Conference was closed.

No. XII. (See page 17.)

Addresses from the Canadian and West Indian Houses of Bishops. 1872 and 1873.

1. To his Grace the President and their Lordships the Bishops of the Upper House of Convocation of Canterbury—

We, the Bishops of the Ecclesiastical Province of Canada, availing ourselves of the opportunity afforded by the meeting of a special Provincial Synod, desire that the following Address, touching the Lambeth

Conference, be forwarded to his Grace, the President, and to the Prolocutor of the Lower House of Convocation of the Province of Canterbury.

We, the Bishops aforesaid, encouraged by the successful results of the Address presented to his Grace the late Archbishop of Canterbury, by the Provincial Synod of Canada, whereby the Lambeth Conference was convened, humbly and earnestly petition that the Convocation of Canterbury will take such action as may seem most expedient to unite with us in requesting the Archbishop of Canterbury to summon a second meeting of the Conference.

We are persuaded that such meeting will be most efficacious in uniting the scattered branches of the Anglican Communion, and in promoting the extension of the Kingdom of Christ throughout the world; and we therefore pray that it may be again convened at the earliest day that may suit the convenience of the Archbishop of Canterbury.

> A. MONTREAL (Metropolitan).
> J. T. ONTARIO.
> J. W. QUEBEC.
> A. H. TORONTO.
> J. HURON.

Montreal, Dec. 13, 1872.

2. "The West Indian Bishops [assembled at Georgetown, Demerara, in 1873] join in the request lately made to the Archbishop of Canterbury by the Bishops of the Canadian Province, that he would summon another meeting of the Bishops of the Anglican Communion throughout the world at as early a date as may seem to his Grace practicable and expedient."

No. XIII. (See page 17.)

Correspondence between Bishops of the Protestant Episcopal Church in the United States and the Archbishop of Canterbury. 1874, 1875.

1. *The Archbishop of Canterbury to Bishop Kerfoot, of Pittsburgh.*

ADDINGTON PARK, CROYDON, *Aug.* 21, 1874.

MY DEAR BISHOP,

Before you leave England, I wish to say to you that the subject of another gathering of Bishops of our Communion at Lambeth has been much talked of lately. If the House of Bishops of your Church were to express their wishes on this subject, it might help me in bringing the matter before my brethren of this country when we meet in January of next year.

Trusting that God will bless you in your journey and on your return to your work,

I am, your faithful Brother,

A. C. CANTUAR.

2. *The Bishop of Pittsburgh to the Archbishop of Canterbury.*

HOUSE OF BISHOPS, NEW YORK, *Nov.* 3, 1874.

MY DEAR LORD,

I had the pleasure not long since of writing to you from this House, to say that the request to your Grace to invite another Lambeth Conference had been signed by forty-three out of forty-six Bishops in attendance. I then said that I would write again fully when the engagements of the General Convention allowed me to do so.

The matter was introduced by me into this House early in our session, so that the Lord Bishop of Lichfield, who was with us for the first week of the Convention, might speak to the Bishops on the subject. He did this with great discretion and effect in our House, and also in the House of Deputies. While the Bishops generally were very favourably disposed towards the proposal (and your Grace's note to me of August 25th very much promoted this inclination), some of them wished that any action of the Bishops should be preceded by some expression from the clerical and lay deputies that would prevent any thought that the Bishops were acting for themselves alone, and not also for and with the clergy and laity. .... It was deemed by all the Bishops to be sufficient, and for several reasons best, that we should express our wish and convey our request to your Grace in the form in which it has by this time reached you through the Bishop of Lichfield. The Bishop of New York and myself prepared the paper, and received the signatures of the Bishops individually. As some of the signatures may not be readily legible, I enclose a printed list of the names of the signers.

It clearly appeared in the consultations of the deputies, and even of the Bishops, that there were not a few misconceptions about the Conference of 1867. This, I think, was due, in large measure, to the misrepresentation of its character and management in the memoir of the late Bishop Hopkins. .... Bishop Hopkins himself would not, I am sure, have approved of the sketch of the Lambeth Conference given by his biographer. But its effects were seen, and I hope counteracted, in the discussions.

In the consultation of the Bishops, the wish was several times expressed that the arrangements for a

Conference in 1876 should be such as to manifest that the variety of the topics admitted, and the time allowed, should be such as would seem to justify a Convocation of our Bishops from all over the world. There was no wish to annex terms or conditions to our request to your Grace. The suggestions already made by the Canadian Synod (whose action on this subject was recited in our House of Bishops) covers most or all of this ground.[1] As our consultations went on, it seemed to be devolved on me, by general consent, to make to you this informal communication about such wishes. Two or three Bishops gave them to me in writing; some others in unwritten words. The thoughts were that the Bishops attending the Conference might propose for discussion such questions as each one should deem right; and that the sessions should be continued long enough to allow of the needful Conferences. Those of us who were at Lambeth seven years ago knew quite well that such were the real character and spirit of that Conference; but that it being then an enterprise and experiment at once novel and anxious, precautions were rightly taken and limitations wisely observed that persons at a distance could not fully or fairly comprehend. The invitation was even then given in advance to the Bishops to suggest topics; and many of us did this, and I believe every such topic was introduced.

I made such answers to the inquiries of some of my brethren, adding that, of course, as then, so whenever we should meet again, no topic should be introduced which must elicit discussions on the State relations of the Church of England. All the Bishops here at once recognise this as the right rule. I said this was the only real limitation I witnessed seven years ago. I ventured to anticipate that on this point every reasonable wish would be satisfied in the future Conference.

[1] See below, page 110.

In thus writing at, I hope, not a needless length to your Grace, I think that I quite fulfil the promises made to some of my American brethren, who united heartily in the request sent to you, and I hope that I also convey such intimations as will entirely meet your own views in your anticipation of any such Conference. I may also add that the careful consideration given to the whole scheme here of late only confirms our convictions of the wisdom and usefulness of the renewal of the Conference of 1867. I am, my dear Lord Archbishop, your Grace's very faithful and affectionate brother.

JOHN B. KERFOOT,
Bishop of Pittsburgh.

3. *The following is the formal Resolution referred to in the foregoing letter.*

The undersigned Bishops of the Protestant Episcopal Church in the United States, having had the pleasure of listening to the statements of the Right Reverend the Lord Bishop of Lichfield, of the Right Reverend the Lord Bishop of Montreal and Metropolitan, of the Right Reverend the Lord Bishop of Kingston, Jamaica, and of the Right Reverend the Lord Bishop of Quebec in reference to the benefits to the whole Anglican Communion to be derived from the holding of another Conference of the Bishops thereof, do most cordially express in their individual capacity their interest in the subject, and their hope that his Grace the Archbishop of Canterbury will find it consistent with his views of duty to take steps towards the assembling of such a Conference.

[The signatures of forty-two Bishops, including the presiding Bishop, are appended.]

4. *The Archbishop of Canterbury to the Bishop of Pittsburgh.*

LAMBETH PALACE, S.W.,
April 27, 1875.

[PRIVATE.]

MY DEAR BISHOP,

As I promised, I brought the question of a second Lambeth Conference and your kind letter before the Bishops of the Southern Province, who met lately in Convocation.

The holding of such a Conference in the autumn of next year is rendered impossible, if not by other causes, by the fact that I find that 1876 is the year in which I must (D.V.) hold my visitation in the autumn, and deliver my charge, and you will understand the impossibility of my undertaking at that time the additional work necessarily involved on so important an occasion as the reassembling of the Lambeth Conference.

We cannot, therefore, look forward to the Conference taking place earlier than 1877, which will be ten years from the time of the first meeting. But, as we know that your Convention meets in the autumn of that year, it appears to us that the Lambeth Conference might well be in the spring of 1877, thus leaving time for our American brethren to return home before this Convention.

I think I ought to add that there was a general impression that, before steps were taken for gathering Bishops from all parts of the world, we ought distinctly to understand what the subjects are on which discussion is desirable. There was a general feeling that matters of doctrine which are already settled by our formularies could not be re-opened, and matters of discipline must be left to the authorities of each separate Church. There remains, therefore, only such general questions as relate to the intercourse of the various branches of our Church, and that brotherly conference which was on former occasions found so valuable.

I write this private letter, as I think you may wish to know the feelings of the English Bishops on this important subject with as little delay as possible, and I hope before long to be able to return a formal answer to the document signed by the Bishops of the American Episcopal Church.

Believe me to be, my dear Bishop,
Very sincerely yours,

A. C. CANTUAR.

5. *To the Right Rev. the Bishops of the Protestant Episcopal Church of the United States of America.*

LAMBETH PALACE, S.E.,
June 7, 1875.

RIGHT REV. AND DEAR BRETHREN,

I have laid before my brethren of the Province of Canterbury your letter on the subject of holding a second Lambeth Conference, and I have had communication on the same subject with the Archbishop of York, as representing the Bishops of the Northern Province.

We entertain a grateful sense of the advantages of that brotherly intercourse which the last Lambeth Conference tended to encourage, and we should look forward with much pleasure to another meeting of the same kind.

I am, however, instructed by my brethren to bring before you the two following considerations, respecting which I should be glad to have your opinion before taking any further steps in this matter.

1. It seems to my brethren and myself that such a

Conference could not with advantage be held till the tenth year after the last meeting. I am aware that this would bring us to the year 1877, in which, as I understand, your general convention holds its triennial meeting; but the autumn of 1876, which has been mentioned by the Bishop of Lichfield as a suitable time, will, so far as I can foresee, be entirely occupied by my visitation of the Archdiocese of Canterbury, and it is the opinion of those whom I have consulted that the most convenient time would be the summer of 1877, say, in the month of July, which time would enable our brethren of the United States to return home for the meeting of their own Convention.

2. I have also been requested to bring before you the following point. You will at once see that I ought not to take the step of inviting so large a body of Bishops to leave the scene of their labours in their distant Dioceses without being able to state to them somewhat explicitly what the practical results are which are expected to be derived from the Conference.

It appears to us that, respecting matters of doctrine, no change can be proposed or discussed, and that no authoritative explanation of doctrine ought to be taken in hand. Each Church is naturally guided in the interpretation of its formularies by its recognised authorities. Again, respecting matters of discipline, each Church has its own appointed Courts for the administration of its ecclesiastical law, with which, of course, such a meeting of Bishops as is proposed claims no power to interfere. The present state of the Christian Church makes men more than usually sensitive as to any appearance even of a claim on the part of any one branch of the Church to interfere with the decisions or administrations of another. Each is considered qualified to regulate its own separate affairs, while all are united in the maintenance of the one faith. Therefore, if the Conference meets, it will be necessary to exclude all questions which might happen to trench on the complete independence of the several branches of the Church.

The propriety of the Bishops meeting in Conference must depend, I conceive, upon this—whether there appear a sufficient number of subjects relating to the brotherly intercourse of the various Branches of the Anglican Communion, on which a conference of the chief Ministers of the several Churches would be likely to throw light.

I should be greatly obliged for any communication which you may be disposed to send to me, during the next six months, as to your views on the general desirableness of our meeting under such circumstances as I have described. I will take care, before the close of the present year, to lay before my brethren in England any statement I receive as to the particular questions which you think it desirable for the Bishops of the Anglican Communion to consider.

This would enable us to come to a decision respecting the Conference, and make any arrangements that may be required.

I remain,
Your faithful brother and servant in Christ,
A. C. CANTUAR.

No. XIV. (See page 18.)

Memorandum of the Canadian House of Bishops. 1874.

Suggestions of the Canadian House of Bishops made to the Bishop of Lichfield concerning the Lambeth Conference.

1. As to the period of its meeting—

We would suggest that 1876 would be a period very convenient and welcome to the Church in Canada.

2. As to the duration of the Conference—

We are of opinion that there should be a continuous Session of one month, four days in each week being days of session ; or,

That there should be at least two weeks of Session, with an interval between the first and last week.

3. As to the matter to be discussed—

We feel that it is most desirable that the Reports of Committees laid before the Conference of 1867 should be carefully considered, with the exception of Report No. 8.

4. We think that it would be very convenient to the Bishops invited to the Congress that an opportunity should be given them of suggesting beforehand any subject which they may wish to have considered.

5. We feel that, if his Grace should be pleased to grant the Bishops an opportunity of assembling in Conference, it would be extremely desirable that his decision on the above matters should be embodied in the Circular of Invitation.

Signed, on behalf of the Bishops of the Province of Canada,

A. MONTREAL, Metropolitan.

No. XV. (See page 20.)

Action of the Convocations of Canterbury and York with reference to the proposed Second Lambeth Conference.

The Memorials from the Canadian and West Indian Bishops (quoted above, No. XII., page 101), were on April 29, 1874, referred by the Upper House of the Convocation of Canterbury to a Joint Committee of fifteen members, who, on July 10, 1874, presented a report in the shape of the following four Resolutions:—

1. "That the relation of his Grace the Lord Archbishop of Canterbury to the other Bishops of the Anglican Communion be that of Primate among Archbishops, Primates, Metropolitans, and Bishops."

2. "That in accordance with the Memorial of the Bishops of the Ecclesiastical Province of Canada, and the resolution of the Bishops of the West Indian Dioceses, his Grace the Lord Archbishop of Canterbury be requested to convene a General Conference of the Bishops of the Anglican Communion to carry on the work begun by the Lambeth Conference in 1867.

3. "That the Reports of Committees presented at the adjourned Session of the Lambeth Conference in 1867, but not adopted or even discussed, be taken into consideration at the Second Conference."

4. "That the Committee recommend that his Grace be respectfully requested to convene the second meeting of the Lambeth Conference for the year 1876."

"G. A. LICHFIELD, Chairman."

The Report was received by the Upper House, and communicated to the Lower House, July 10, 1874.—(*See Chronicle of Convocation, pp.* 437–439.)

The Upper House of Canterbury Convocation had also resolved, on April 29, 1874, to invite an expression of opinion from the Convocation of York, and that Convocation, on February 26, 1875, passed the following resolution:—

"That this Synod, in reply to a communication from the Province of Canterbury, asking for an expression of opinion upon three resolutions respecting certain memorials received from the Ecclesiastical Province of Canada, and from the Bishops of the West Indian Dioceses, prays that his Grace the President will convey to his Grace the Archbishop of Canterbury the wish of this Synod that all necessary steps may be taken for the assembling of a second Conference at Lambeth, but would desire to leave all other questions involved in these resolutions to be decided as may seem best to the Archbishops and the bench of Bishops."

No. XVI.   (See page 20.)

Circular Letter of Inquiry addressed by the Archbishop of Canterbury to all the Anglican Bishops, March 28, 1876.

LAMBETH PALACE, *March* 28, 1876.

RIGHT REVEREND BROTHER,

A wish has been expressed by many Bishops of the Protestant Episcopal Church in the United States of America, by the Bishops of the Canadian Dominion, and by the West Indian Bishops, that a second Conference of our brethren should be held at Lambeth.

Before I decide upon the important step of inviting the Bishops of our Communion throughout the world to assemble at Lambeth, I have thought it right, after consultation with the Bishops of England, to give all our brethren an opportunity of expressing their opinion upon the expediency of convening such a Conference at this time, and upon the choice of the subjects which ought to engage its attention, if it be convened.

I therefore beg leave to intimate to you our readiness to hold a Conference at Lambeth in or about the month of July, 1878, if it shall seem expedient, after the opinions of all our brethren have been ascertained; and I need scarcely assure you that your advice is earnestly desired, and will be respectfully considered. May I ask, for our guidance, whether you are willing, and are likely to be able, to attend the Conference yourself?

Those who were present at Lambeth in 1867 thankfully acknowledged that, through the blessing of Almighty God, the Bishops of the various branches of the Anglican Communion were drawn together in closer bonds of brotherly love and sympathy.

The help and comfort which are due from the branches of Christ's Church to each other are more readily rendered, and more fully each is made acquainted with the wants of the rest. In this time of religious activity and increased intercourse between all parts of the world, there is greater need than ever of mutual counsel amongst the Bishops of our widely-extended Communion.

The Bishops of England, therefore, earnestly ask you to join with them in prayer that we may all be guided to a wise decision on this important matter, and if it should be resolved to hold the Conference, that its deliberations may issue in greater peace, and strength, and energy to the whole Church of Christ.

Anxiously awaiting your answer,

I remain,

Your faithful Brother and Servant in Christ,

A. C. CANTUAR.

The Right Reverend the Bishop of . . . . .

"Covering letter" to the Metropolitans and Presiding Bishops.

LAMBETH PALACE, S.E., *March* 28, 1876.

MY DEAR BISHOP,

After consultation with my Brethren the Bishops of England, including the Archbishop of York, I beg leave to address you as   of [1] and request you to circulate among the Bishops of your branch of the Church the enclosed documents, having reference to a second Lambeth Conference.

I shall feel obliged by your favouring us at your earliest convenience with your own views on the questions now submitted to your consideration.

I remain your faithful brother and servant in Christ.

A. C. CANTUAR.

No. XVII.   (See page 21.)

Letter of Invitation to the Conference of 1878.

LAMBETH PALACE, *July* 10, 1877.

RIGHT REVEREND AND DEAR BROTHER,

It is proposed to hold a Conference of Bishops of the Anglican Communion at this place, beginning on Tuesday, the second day of July, Eighteen hundred and Seventy-eight.

The Conference, it is proposed, shall extend over four weeks; the first week of four Sessions to be devoted to discussions, in Conference, of the subjects submitted for deliberation; the second and third

---

[1] *e.g.*, Metropolitan of Canada.

weeks to the consideration of these subjects in Committees ; and the fourth week to final discussions in Conference, and to the close of the Meeting.

The subjects selected for discussion are the following :—

1. The best mode of maintaining Union among the various Churches of the Anglican Communion.

2. Voluntary Boards of Arbitration for Churches to which such an arrangement may be applicable.

3. The relations to each other of Missionary Bishops and of Misionaries in various branches of the Anglican Communion acting in the same country.

4. The position of Anglican Chaplains and Chaplaincies on the continent of Europe and elsewhere.

5. Modern forms of infidelity, and the best means of dealing with them.

6. The condition, progress, and needs of the various Churches of the Anglican Communion.

I shall feel greatly obliged if, at your early convenience, you will inform me whether we may have the pleasure of expecting your presence at the Conference.

I am, Right Reverend and dear brother, yours faithfully in Christ.

A. C. CANTUAR.

No. XVIII. (See page 28.)

Letter of the Bishops attending the Lambeth Conference of 1878, including the Reports adopted by the Conference.

CONTENTS.

Introductory ... ... *page*	118
Report of Committee on "The best mode of maintaining Union among the various Churches of the Anglican Communion"	118
Report of Committee on "Voluntary Boards of Arbitration for Churches to which such an arrangement may be applicable"	125
Report of Committee on "The relation to each other of Missionary Bishops and of Missionaries of various branches of the Anglican Communion, acting in the same country"	128
Report of Committee on "The position of Anglican Chaplains and Chaplaincies on the Continent of Europe and elsewhere"...	133
Report of Committee appointed to receive questions submitted to them, in writing, by Bishops desiring the advice of the Conference on difficulties or problems they have met with in their several Dioceses, and to report thereon	134
Conclusion	140
Notes	141

LETTER.

TO THE FAITHFUL IN CHRIST JESUS, GREETING—

We, Archbishops, Bishops, Metropolitan, and other Bishops of the Holy Catholic Church, in full communion with the Church of England, one hundred in number, all exercising superintendence over Dioceses, or lawfully commissioned to exercise Episcopal functions therein, assembled, many of us from the most distant parts of the earth, at Lambeth Palace, in the year of our Lord 1878, under the presidency of the most reverend Archibald Campbell, by Divine Providence Archbishop of Canterbury, Primate of all England; after receiving, in the private Chapel of the said Palace, the blessed Sacrament of the Lord's Body and Blood, and after having united in prayer for the guidance of the Holy Spirit, have taken into our consideration various definite questions submitted to us affecting the condition of the Church in divers parts of the world,

We have made these questions the subject of serious deliberation for many days, and we now commend to the faithful the conclusions which have been adopted.

Report of Committee on the best mode of maintaining union among the various Churches of the Anglican Communion.

1.—In considering the best mode of maintaining union among the various Churches of our Communion, the Committee, first of all, recognise, with deep thankfulness to Almighty God, the essential and evident unity in which the Church of England and the Churches in visible communion with her have always been bound together.[1] United under One Divine Head in the fellowship of the One Catholic and Apostolic Church, holding the One Faith revealed in Holy Writ, defined in the Creeds, and maintained by the Primitive Church, receiving the same Canonical Scriptures of the Old and New Testaments as containing all things necessary to salvation—these Churches teach the same Word of God, partake of the same divinely-ordained Sacraments, through the ministry of the same Apostolic orders, and worship one God and Father through the same Lord Jesus Christ, by the same Holy and Divine Spirit, Who is given to those that believe, to guide them into all truth.

2.—Together with this unity, however, there has existed among these Churches that variety of custom, discipline, and form of worship which necessarily results from the exercise by each "particular or national Church" of its right "to ordain, change, and abolish ceremonies or rites of the Church ordained only by man's authority, so that all things be done to edifying." We gladly acknowledge that there is at present no real ground for anxiety on account of this diversity; but the desire has of late been largely felt and expressed, that some practical and efficient methods should be adopted, in order to guard against possible sources of disunion in the future, and at the same time further to manifest and cherish that true and substantial agreement which exists among these increasingly numerous Churches.

3.—The method which first naturally suggests itself is that which, originating with the inspired Apostles, long served to hold all the Churches of Christ in one undivided and visible communion. The assembling, however, of a true General Council, such as the Church of England has always declared her readiness to resort to, is, in the present condition of Christen-

---

[1] Note A, p. 141.

dom, unhappily but obviously impossible. The difficulties attending the assembling of a Synod of all the Anglican Churches, though different in character and less serious in nature, seem to us nevertheless too great to allow of our recommending it for present adoption.

4.—The experiment, now twice tried, of a Conference of Bishops called together by the Archbishop of Canterbury, and meeting under his presidency, offers at least the hope that the problem, hitherto unsolved, of combining together for consultation representatives of Churches so differently situated and administered, may find, in the providential course of events, its own solution.[1] Your Committee would, on this point, venture to suggest that such Conferences, called together from time to time by the Archbishop of Canterbury, at the request of, or in consultation with, the Bishops of our Communion, might with advantage be invested in future with somewhat larger liberty as to the initiation and selection of subjects for discussion. For example, a Committee might be constituted, such as should represent, more or less completely, the several Churches of the Anglican Communion; and to this Committee it might be entrusted to draw up, after receiving communications from the Bishops, a scheme of subjects to be discussed.

5.—Meanwhile, there are certain principles of Church order which, your Committee consider, ought to be distinctly recognized and set forth, as of great importance for the maintenance of union among the Churches of our Communion.

(1.) First, that the duly-certified action of every national or particular Church, and of each ecclesiastical Province (or Diocese not included in a Province), in the exercise of its own discipline, should be

---

[1] Note B, p. 142.

respected by all the other Churches, and by their individual members.

(2.) Secondly, that when a Diocese, or territorial sphere of administration, has been constituted by the authority of any Church or Province of this Communion within its own limits, no Bishop or other Clergyman of any other Church should exercise his functions within that Diocese without the consent of the Bishop thereof.[1]

(3.) Thirdly, that no Bishop should authorize to officiate in his Diocese a clergyman coming from another Church or Province, unless such Clergyman present letters testimonial, countersigned by the Bishop of the Diocese from which he comes; such letters to be, as nearly as possible, in the form adopted by such Church or Province in the case of the transfer of a clergyman from one Diocese to another.

Passing to details, your Committee would call attention to the following points:—

I.—*Of Church Organization*

6.—Inasmuch as the sufficient and effective organization of the several parts of the Church tends to promote the unity of the whole, your Committee would, with this view, repeat the recommendation in the sixth report of the first Lambeth Conference,[2] that those Dioceses which still remain isolated should, as circumstances may allow, associate themselves into a Province or Provinces, in accordance with the ancient laws and usages of the Catholic Church.

---

[1] This does not refer to questions respecting missionary Bishops and foreign chaplaincies, which have been entrusted to other Committees.

[2] Note C, p. 145.

II.—*Of Common Work.*

7.—Believing that the unity of our Churches will be especially manifested and strengthened by their uniting together in common work, your Committee would call attention to the great value of such co-operation wherever the opportunity shall present itself; as, for example, in founding and maintaining, in the missionary fields, schools for the training of a native ministry, such as that which is now contemplated in Shanghai, and, generally, as far as may be possible, in prosecuting missionary work, such as that which the Churches in England and Scotland are maintaining together in Kaffraria.

III.—*Of Commendatory Letters.*

8—(1.) This Committee would renew the recommendation of the first Lambeth Conference, that letters commendatory should be given by their own Bishops to clergymen visiting for a time other Churches than those to which they belong.

(2). They would urge yet more emphatically the importance of letters commendatory being given by their own clergymen to members of their flocks going from one country to another. And they consider it desirable that the clergy should urge on such persons the duty of promptly presenting these letters, and should carefully instruct them as to the oneness of the Church in its Apostolical constitution under its varying organization and conditions.

It may not, perhaps, be considered foreign to this subject to suggest here the importance of impressing upon our people the extent and geographical distribution of our Churches, and of reminding them that there is now hardly any part of the world where members of our Communion may not find a Church one with their own in faith, order, and worship.

IV.—*Of circulating Information as to the Churches.*

9.—It appears that the want has been much felt of some centre of communication among the Churches in England, Ireland, Scotland, America, India, the Colonies, and elsewhere, through which ecclesiastical documents of importance might be mutually circulated, and in which copies of them might be retained for reference. Your Committee would suggest that the Society for Promoting Christian Knowledge might be requested to maintain a department for this purpose, supported by special contributions; and also that provision might be made for the more general dissemination in each Church of information respecting the acts and current history of all the rest. They recommend that the Reports and other proceedings of this Conference, which it may think fit to publish, should be communicated through this channel. They further think it desirable that the official acts, and other published documents of each representative body of this Communion, should be interchanged among the respective Bishops and the officers of such bodies.

V.—*Of a Day of Intercession.*

10.—Remembering the blessing promised to united intercession, and believing that such intercession ever tends to deepen and strengthen that unity of His Church for which Our Lord earnestly pleaded in His great intercessory prayer, your Committee trust that this Conference will give the weight of its recommendation to the observance throughout the Churches of this Communion of a season of prayer for the unity of Christendom. This recommendation has been, to some extent, anticipated by the practice adopted of late years of setting apart a Day of Intercession for Missions. Your Committee would by no means wish to interfere with an observance which appears to have been widely accepted, and signally blessed of God. But, as our Divine Lord has so closely connected the unity of His followers with the world's belief in His own Mission from the Father, it seems to us that intercessions for the enlargement of His Kingdom may well be joined with earnest prayer that all who profess faith in Him may be one flock under one Shepherd. With respect to the day, your Committee have been informed that the Festival of St. Andrew, hitherto observed as the Day of Intercession for Missions, is found to be unsuitable to the circumstances of the Church in many parts of the world. They, therefore, venture to suggest that, after the present year, the time selected should be the Tuesday before Ascension Day (being a Rogation Day), or any of the seven days after that Tuesday; and they hope that all the Bishops of the several Churches will commend this observance to their respective Dioceses.

VI.—*Of Diversities in Worship.*

11.—Your Committee, believing that, next to oneness in "the Faith once delivered to the saints," communion in worship is the link which most firmly binds together bodies of Christian men, and remembering that the book of Common Prayer, retained as it is, with some modifications, by all our Churches, has been one principal bond of union among them, desire to call attention to the fact that such communion in worship may be endangered by excessive diversities of ritual. They believe that the internal unity of the several Churches will help greatly to the union of these one with another. And, while they consider that such large elasticity in the forms of worship is desirable as will give wide scope to all legitimate expressions of devotional feeling, they would appeal, on the other hand, to the Apostolic precept that " all things be done unto edifying," and to the Catholic principle that order and obedience, even at the sacrifice of personal preferences and tastes, lie at the foundation of Christian unity, and are even essential to the successful maintenance of the Faith.

12.—They cannot leave this subject without expressing an earnest hope that Churchmen of all views, however varying, will recognise the duty of submitting themselves, for conscience sake, in matters ritual and ceremonial, to the authoritative judgments of that particular or national Church in which, by God's Providence, they may be placed; and that they will abstain from all that tends to estrangement or irritation, and will rather daily and fervently pray that the Holy Spirit may guide every member of the Church to "think and do always such things as be rightful," and that He may unite us all in that brotherly charity which is " the very bond of peace and of all virtues."

Report of Committee on Voluntary Boards of Arbitration for Churches to which such an arrangement may be applicable:

1.—Your Committee beg to submit the following Report :—

2.—The necessity for considering the subject which is entrusted to your Committee—namely, Voluntary Boards of Arbitration for Churches to which such an arrangement may be applicable—has arisen from the fact that there is no appeal from the Ecclesiastical Tribunals in the Colonial Churches to any of the ordinary Ecclesiastical Courts of England, or to the Judicial Committee of the Privy Council, when advising Her Majesty on appeals from Ecclesiastical Courts. No questions relating to the exercise of discipline in a Colonial Church can come before the Judicial Committee of the Privy Council, except on appeal from Civil Courts in the colony, exercising jurisdiction in matters affecting property or civil rights. The subject, therefore, before your Committee is not the constitution or jurisdiction of Provincial or Diocesan tribunals, but whether there should be some external tribunals or "Voluntary Boards of Arbitration" to which an appeal or reference ought to be made ; how such Boards, when necessary, should be constituted ; and under what circumstances they should be approached.

3.—Your Committee, having taken into consideration the whole question, especially with reference to the action of some of the Colonial Churches since 1867, when a Report bearing upon this subject was prepared by a Committee of the Lambeth Conference held in that year, would make the following general recommendations :—

4.—I. (*a*) Every Ecclesiastical Province, which has constituted for the exercise of discipline over its clergy a tribunal for receiving appeals from its Diocesan Courts, should be held responsible for its own decisions in the exercise of such discipline ; and your Committee are not prepared to recommend that there should be any one central tribunal of appeal from such Provincial tribunals.

5.—(*b*) If any Province is desirous that its tribunals of appeal should have power to obtain, in matters of doctrine, or of discipline involving a question of doctrine, the opinion of some council of reference before pronouncing sentence, your Committee consider that the conditions of such reference must be determined by the Province itself ; but that the opinion of the council should be given on a consideration of the facts of the case, sent up to it in writing by the tribunal of appeal, and not merely on an abstract question of doctrine.

6.—(*c*) In Dioceses which have not yet been combined into a Province, or which may be geographically incapable of being so combined, your Committee recommend that appeals should lie from the Diocesan Courts to the Archbishop of Canterbury, to be heard by his Grace with such assistance as he may deem best. The circumstances of each Diocese must determine how such consensual jurisdiction could be enforced.

7.—II. As regards the very grave question of the trial of a Bishop, inasmuch as any tribunal, constituted for this purpose by a Province, is necessarily a tribunal of first instance, it would, in the opinion of your Committee, be expedient that, when any such provisions can be introduced by voluntary compact into the constitutions or canons of any Church, the following conditions should be observed :—

8.—(*a*) When any Bishop shall have been sentenced by the tribunal constituted for the trial of a Bishop in any Ecclesiastical Province, if no Bishop of the Province, other than the accused, shall dissent from the judgment, there should be no appeal, provided that the case be heard by not fewer than five Bishops, who shall be unanimous in their judgment.

9.—(*b*) If, in consequence of the small number of Bishops in a Province, or from any other sufficient cause, a tribunal of five comprovincial Bishops cannot be formed, your Committee would suggest that the Province should provide for the enlargement of the tribunal by the addition of Bishops from a neighbouring Province.

10.—(*c*) In the event of the Provincial tribunal not fulfilling the conditions indicated in paragraph 8 of this Report, your Committee would suggest that, whenever an external tribunal of appeal is not provided in the Canons of that Province, it should be in the power of the accused Bishop, if condemned, to require the Provincial tribunal to refer the case to at least five Metropolitans or chief Bishops of the Anglican Communion to be named in the said

Canons, of whom the Archbishop of Canterbury should be one ; and that, if any three of these shall require that the case, or any portion of it, shall be re-heard or reviewed, it should be so re-heard or reviewed.

11.—(*d*) In cases in which an Ecclesiastical Province desires to have a tribunal of appeal from its Provincial tribunal for trying a Bishop, your Committee consider that such tribunal should consist of not less than five Bishops of the Churches of the Anglican Communion, under the presidency of the Archbishop of Canterbury, if his Grace will consent thereto, with the assistance of laymen learned in the law.

Report of Committee on the relation to each other of Missionary Bishops and of Missionaries of various branches of the Anglican Communion acting in the same country.

1.—Your Committee beg to submit the following Report :—

I.

2.—Your Committee have had before them the question of providing Books of Common Prayer for converts from heathenism, suitable to the special wants of various countries ; and they recommend as follows :—

3.—They think it very important that such books should not be introduced or multiplied without proper authority ; and, since grave inconvenience might follow the use of different Prayer Books in the same district, in English and American Missions, they recommend that, whenever it is possible, one Prayer Book only should be in use.

4.—It is expedient that Books of Common Prayer, suitable to the needs of native congregations in heathen countries, should be framed : that the principles embodied in such books should be identical with the principles embodied in the Book of Common Prayer; and that the deviations from the Book of Common Prayer in point of form should only be such as are required by the circumstances of particular churches.

5.—In the case of heathen countries not under English or American rule, any such book should be approved by a Board consisting of the Bishop or Bishops under whose authority the book is intended to be used, and of certain clergymen, not less than three where possible, from the diocese or dioceses, or district, and should then be communicated by such Bishop or Bishops, or by the Metropolitan of the province to which any such Bishop belongs, to a Board in England, consisting of the Archbishops of England and Ireland, the Bishop of London, the Primus of the Scottish Episcopal Church, together with two Bishops and four clergymen selected by them, and also to a Board appointed by the General Convention of the Protestant Episcopal Church in the United States of America.

6.—No such book should be held to have been authorised for use in public worship unless it have received the sanction of these two Boards.

7.—In any Diocese of a country under English rule all such new books, being modifications or versions of the Book of Common Prayer, should be submitted, after approval by local authority, to the Board in England only.

II.

8.—Your Committee have considered the case of Missions in countries not under English or American rule, and they recommend as follows:—

9.—In cases where two Bishops of the Anglican Communion are ministering in the same country, as in China, Japan, and Western Africa at the present time, your Committee are of opinion that under existing circumstances each Bishop should have control of his own clergy, and their converts and congregations.

10.—The various Bishops in the same country should endeavour, as members of the same Communion, to keep up brotherly intercourse with each other on the subject of their Missionary work.

11.—In countries not under English or American rule, the English or American Church would not ordinarily undertake to establish Dioceses with strictly-defined territorial limits; although either Church might indicate the district in which it was intended that the Missionary Bishop should labour.

12.—Bishops in the same country should take care not to interfere in any manner with the congregations or converts of each other.

13.—It is most undesirable that either Church should for the future send a Bishop or Missionaries to a town or district already occupied by a Bishop of another branch of the Anglican Communion.

14.—When it is intended to send forth any new Missionary Bishop, notification of such an intention should be sent beforehand to the Archbishop of Canterbury, to the Presiding Bishop of the Protestant Episcopal Church in the United States of America, and to the Metropolitan of any Province near which the Missionary Bishop is to minister.

III.

15.—Your Committee have had before them a communication from the Bishop of Calcutta, dated June 4th, 1878, containing Resolutions of the Bishops of India and Ceylon, also a letter from Bishop Caldwell, dated June 1st, 1878, on the subject of the relation of Bishops abroad to the Missionaries in their Dioceses or districts.

16.—The questions raised by the Bishop of Calcutta's communication relate to the power and authority of the Bishop in respect of giving and withdrawing the licences, 1st, of the clergy under his charge; 2nd, of lay readers and catechists; also to the rights of the Bishop in reference to changes in the management, order of service, and place of worship of any congregation.

17.—As regards the licensing of the clergy, it is admitted generally that every Missionary clergyman, whether appointed by a society or otherwise, should receive the licence of the Bishop in whose Diocese he is to labour; but your Committee are of opinion that, in case of refusal to give a licence to a clergyman, the Bishop should, if the clergyman desire it, state the reasons of his refusal, and transmit them to the Metropolitan, who should have power to decide upon their sufficiency; such reasons should also be accessible to the person whose licence is in question. Where there is no Metropolitan, the reasons should be transmitted to the Archbishop of Canterbury, who should decide in like manner.

18.—As regards the withdrawal of a licence, your Committee find that in some Provinces the mode of proceeding for revocation has been fixed by canon, and the jurisdiction thus created has been established by consent. For these places it is not necessary to make any recommendations. Where no such jurisdiction exists, your Committee recommend that the Bishop should in no case proceed to the revocation of a clergyman's licence without affording him the opportunity of showing cause against it, and that if the Bishop shall afterwards proceed to revoke the licence, he should, if the clergyman desire it, state the reasons for his decision to such clergyman, and also to the Metropolitan, who should have power to sanction or disallow the revocation. In cases where there is no Metropolitan, the Archbishop of Canterbury should be regarded as the Metropolitan for this purpose. No such revocation should take place, except for grave ecclesiastical offences.

19.—The Bishop would probably find it desirable, where the clergyman is connected with one of the great Missionary societies, to communicate with the society, or its local representatives, before taking steps for revocation of a licence.

20.—With regard to lay agents, your Committee consider it desirable that such as are employed in more important spiritual functions should have the licence, or other express sanction of the Bishop ; and that other laymen employed in Missionary work should be considered to have the implied sanction of the Bishop, and should not continue to be so employed, if the Bishop see fit, for a grave reason, to forbid them.

21.—The authority of the Bishop in appointing places for public worship has been always admitted in the Church. Every place in which the Holy Communion is regularly celebrated should have the sanction of the Bishop.

22.—Your Committee have been asked for an opinion as to Subordinate, Co-ordinate, or Suffragan Bishops in India, to minister to native congregations, within the limits of another Diocese. Your Committee think that there are manifest objections to the appointment of a Bishop to minister to certain congregations within the Diocese of another Bishop, and wholly independent of him. Your Committee think that, for the present, the appointment of Assistant Bishops, whether European or native, subordinate to the Bishop of the Diocese, would meet the special needs of India in this matter, and would offer the best security for order and peace.

Report of Committee on the position of Anglican Chaplains and Chaplaincies on the Continent of Europe and elsewhere.

1.—Your Committee have to report that they have agreed to the following recommendations:—

2.—I. That it is highly desirable that Anglican congregations, on the Continent of Europe and elsewhere, should be distinctly urged not to admit the stated ministrations of any clergyman without the written licence or permission of the Bishop of the Anglican Communion who is duly authorised to grant it; and that the occasional assistance of strangers should not be invited or permitted without some satisfactory evidence of their ordination and character as clergymen.

3.—II. That it is desirable, as a general rule, that two chapels shall not be established where one is sufficient for the members of both Churches, American and English; also that where there is only one church or chapel the members of both Churches should be represented on the Committee, if any.

4.—III. That it be suggested to the Societies which partly support Continental Chaplaincies, that, in places where English and American churchmen reside or visit, and especially where Americans outnumber the English, it may be desirable to appoint a properly-accredited clergyman of the American Church.

5.—IV. That your Committee, having carefully considered a Memorial addressed to the Archbishops and Bishops of the Church of England by four Priests and certain other members of "the Spanish and Portuguese Reformed Episcopal Church," praying for the consecration of a Bishop, cannot but express their hearty sympathy with the Memorialists in the difficulties of their position; and, having heard a statement on the subject of the proposed extension of the Episcopate to Mexico by the American Church, they venture to suggest that, when a Bishop shall have been consecrated by the American Church for Mexico, he might be induced to visit Spain and Portugal, and render such assistance at this stage of the movement as may seem to him practicable and advisable.

Report of Committee appointed to receive questions submitted to them, in writing, by Bishops desiring the advice of the Conference on difficulties or problems they have met with in their several Dioceses, and to report thereon.

Attention has been called to the following subjects by questions submitted to your Committee :—

A.

1.—The position which the Anglican Church should assume towards the "Old Catholics" and towards other persons on the Continent of Europe who have renounced their allegiance to the Church of Rome, and who are desirous of forming some connection with the Anglican Church, either English or American.

2.—Applications for intercommunion between themselves and the Anglican Church from persons connected with the Armenian and other Christian communities in the East.

3.—The position of Moravian ministers within the territorial limits of Dioceses of the Anglican Communion.

B.

1.—The West Indian Dioceses.
   (*a*) Their proposed Provincial organization.
   (*b*) The position of their Diaconate.
2.—The Church of Haiti.

C.

Local peculiarities regarding the Laws of Marriage.

D.

A Board of Reference for matters connected with Foreign Missions.

E.

Difficulties arising in the Church of England from the revival of obsolete forms of Ritual, and from erroneous teaching on the subject of Confession.

A.

The fact that a solemn protest is raised in so many Churches and Christian communities throughout the world against the usurpations of the See of Rome, and against the novel doctrines promulgated by its authority, is a subject for thankfulness to Almighty God. All sympathy is due from the Anglican Church to the Churches and individuals protesting against these errors, and labouring, it may be, under special difficulties from the assaults of unbelief as well as from the pretensions of Rome.

We acknowledge but one Mediator between God and men—the Man Christ Jesus, Who is over all, God blessed for ever. We reject, as contrary to the Scriptures and to Catholic truth, any doctrine which would set up other mediators in His place, or which would take away from the Divine Majesty of the fulness of the Godhead which dwelleth in Him, and which gave an infinite value to the spotless Sacrifice which He offered, once for all, on the Cross for the sins of the whole world.

It is therefore our duty to warn the faithful that the act done by the Bishop of Rome, in the Vatican Council, in the year 1870—whereby he asserted a supremacy over all men in matters both of faith and morals, on the ground of an assumed infallibility—was an invasion of the attributes of the Lord Jesus Christ.

The principles on which the Church of England has reformed itself are well known. We proclaim the sufficiency and supremacy of the Holy Scriptures as the ultimate rule of faith, and commend to our people the diligent study of the same. We confess our faith in the words of the ancient Catholic creeds. We retain the Apostolic order of Bishops, Priests, and Deacons. We assert the just liberties of particular or national Churches. We provide our people, in their own tongue, with a Book of Common Prayer and Offices for the administration of the Sacraments, in accordance with the best and most ancient types of Christian faith and worship. These documents are before the world, and can be known and read of all men. We gladly welcome every effort for reform upon the model of the Primitive Church. We do not demand a rigid uniformity; we deprecate needless divisions; but to those who are drawn to us in the endeavour to free themselves from the yoke of error and superstition we are ready to offer all help, and such privileges as may be acceptable to them and are consistent with the maintenance of our own principles as enunciated in our formularies.

Your Committee recommend that questions of the class now submitted to them be dealt with in this spirit. For the consideration, however, of any definite cases in which advice and assistance may, from time to time, be sought, your Committee recommend that the Archbishops of England and Ireland, with the Bishop of London, the Primus of the Scottish Episcopal Church, and the Presiding Bishop of the Protestant Episcopal Church in the United States of America, the Bishop superintending the congregations of the same upon the Continent of Europe, and the Bishop of Gibraltar, together with such other Bishops as they may associate with themselves, be requested to advise upon such cases as circumstances may require.

With regard to the special questions now raised respecting Moravian Orders,[1] the above-mentioned prelates are recommended to associate with themselves such learned persons as they may deem eminently qualified to assist them by their knowledge of the historical difficulties involved.

B.

1.—(a) With respect to the West Indian Dioceses, assuming such Dioceses to desire to be combined into a Province, your Committee advise that the formal consent of the Diocesan Representative Synods, if free (as regards their relation to the State) to give such consent, be first obtained.

The Bishops of the several Dioceses would then forward such formal consent, or expressed desire, to the Archbishop of Canterbury, requesting him to give his sanction to the formation of the Province.

Whether the General Synod of the Province should consist of the Bishops, with representatives of the

---

[1] The special questions submitted were the following :—

"1. If a Moravian presbyter or deacon desires to be received into the Anglican Ministry, ought I to (a) ordain him absolutely ; (b) reordain him conditionally ; (c) accept his orders as valid, and simply give him mission in the Anglican Church?

"2. Can I canonically and regularly commission a Bishop of the Unitas Fratrum in my Diocese either to confirm or to ordain for me, or to do both Episcopal acts according to the Anglican ritual?

"3. Am I justified, if called on, to confirm children, or ordain presbyters or deacons, or do both for the Moravians, in their churches, and according to their ritual?

"4. May Anglican presbyters and deacons, with their Bishop's sanction, officiate and minister the sacraments in Moravian churches, according to their ritual, and invite Moravian presbyters or deacons to execute the functions appertaining to their office in Anglican churches, and according to Anglican ritual?"

clergy and laity of the respective Dioceses, or should consist of the Bishops of the Province only ; and, in the latter case, what limitation should be imposed on the powers of such purely Episcopal Synod, is a question which ought to be left to the Diocesan Synods to decide, with the approval of the Archbishop of Canterbury.

If the West Indian Dioceses be formed into a Province, it seems desirable that a Metropolitan should be, in the first instance, elected from and by the Bishops of the West Indian Dioceses.

(*b*) The questions[1] submitted respecting the peculiar circumstances of the West Indian Diaconate appear to your Committee, upon full consideration, to be such as can be adequately decided only in Diocesan or Provincial Synods.

2.—Your Committee desire to express their satisfaction on learning that a Church in connexion with the Anglican Communion has been planted in the island of Haiti ; that a Bishop has been consecrated thereto by Bishops of the Protestant Episcopal Church in the United States of America, and the Bishop of Kingston, Jamaica ; and that successful efforts are being made for the training of a native Ministry ; and your Committee trust that God's blessing may rest upon the Bishop, Priests, and Deacons, and all other members of this Church.

---

[1] These questions raised the following points :—

1. The desirableness, or otherwise, of recognising a Diaconate which, in certain cases, shall be practically permanent, instead of regarding the Diaconate as the invariable step to the Presbyterate.

2. The desirableness, or otherwise, of permitting Deacons to engage in such secular callings as are not inconsistent with the due and edifying discharge of sacred functions.

3. What modifications, if any, should be allowed as regards the intellectual qualifications and tests to be required of, and imposed on, such laymen as desire to become Deacons without relinquishing their secular vocation.

C.

With regard to those questions in connexion with the Laws of Marriage which have been submitted to them, your Committee, while fully recognising the difficulties in which various branches of the Church have been placed by the action of local Legislatures, are of opinion that steps should be taken by each branch of the Church, according to its own discretion, to maintain the sanctity of marriage, agreeably to the principles set forth in the Word of God, as the Church of Christ hath hitherto received the same.

D.

With respect to what has been submitted to us on the subject of Foreign Missions, your Committee are of opinion that it is desirable to appoint a Board of Reference, to advise upon questions brought before it either by Diocesan or Missionary Bishops or by Missionary Societies. Your Committee are further of opinion that the details of the formation and constitution of such Board ought to be referred to the Archbishops of England and Ireland, the Bishop of London, the Primus of the Scottish Episcopal Church, the Presiding Bishop of the Protestant Episcopal Church in the United States of America, with the Bishop superintending the congregations of the same upon the Continent of Europe, and such other Bishops as they may associate with themselves, who should communicate with the authorities of the various Colonial Churches, and with the existing Missionary Organisations of the Anglican Communion.

E.

Considering unhappy disputes on questions of ritual, whereby divers congregations in the Church of England and elsewhere have been seriously disquieted, your Committee desire to affirm the principle that no alteration from long-accustomed ritual should be made contrary to the admonition of the Bishop of the Diocese.

Further, having in view certain novel practices and teachings on the subject of Confession, your Committee desire to affirm that in the matter of Confession the Churches of the Anglican Communion hold fast those principles which are set forth in the Holy Scriptures, which were professed by the Primitive Church, and which were re-affirmed at the English Reformation; and it is their deliberate opinion that no minister of the Church is authorised to require from those who may resort to him to open their grief a particular or detailed enumeration of all their sins, or to require private confession previous to receiving the Holy Communion, or to enjoin or even encourage the practice of habitual confession to a Priest, or to teach that such practice of habitual confession, or the being subject to what has been termed the direction of a Priest, is a condition of attaining to the highest spiritual life. At the same time your Committee are not to be understood as desiring to limit in any way the provision made in the Book of Common Prayer for the relief of troubled consciences.

These are the Reports of the Conference, and the practical conclusions at which we have arrived. Some of these conclusions have reference to the special circumstances of different branches of the One Church of Christ, according to peculiarities of their various Missionary work for the heathen, or their labours amongst their own people; some embody principles which apply to all branches of the Church Universal. They are all limited in their scope to those subjects which have been distinctly brought before the assembled Bishops. We invite to them the attention of the various Synods and other governing powers in the several Churches, and of all the faithful in Christ Jesus throughout the world.

We do not claim to be lords over God's heritage, but we commend the results of this our Conference to the reason and conscience of our brethren as enlightened by the Holy Spirit of God, praying that all throughout the world who call upon the name of our Lord Jesus Christ may be of one mind, may be united in one fellowship, may hold fast the Faith once delivered to the saints, and worship their one Lord in the spirit of purity and love.

Signed, on behalf of the Conference,

A. C. CANTUAR.

C. J. GLOUCESTER AND BRISTOL,
Secretary of the Conference.

HENRY, BISHOP OF EDINBURGH,
Secretary of Committees.

I. BRUNEL, Chancellor of the Diocese of Ely,
Assistant Secretary.

NOTE A (page 119).

The Churches thus united are, at this time, the Church of England and the Churches planted by her in India, the Colonies, and elsewhere, most of which Churches are associated into distinct Provinces[1]; the Church of Ireland; the Episcopal

---

[1] There are six Provinces, viz. :—
    India, with six Dioceses.
    Canada, with nine Dioceses.
    Rupertsland, with four Dioceses.
    South Africa, with eight Dioceses.
    Australia, with twelve Dioceses.
    New Zealand, with seven Dioceses.
And there are twenty Dioceses not yet associated in Provinces

Church in Scotland; the Protestant Episcopal Church in the United States of America, with its Missionary Branches; and the Church in Haiti. Among the external evidences of the unity of these Churches, none is more significant than that which frequently occurs—the uniting of Bishops of different Churches, *e.g.*, of English, Scottish, and American Bishops, in that most important function by which the Episcopal succession is continued. On more than one occasion, also, the Church in Scotland has consecrated a Bishop in behalf of the Church of England, when legal difficulties have impeded the consecration in England.

NOTE B (page 120).

One of the results of the first Lambeth Conference was the appointment of a Committee to prepare a Bill for placing on a more satisfactory footing the status in England of clergy ordained by Bishops of Colonial and other Churches outside the Church in England.

A Bill to effect this object was introduced by Lord Blachford into Parliament in the Session of 1873, and became law in the Session of 1874, under the name of "The Colonial Clergy Act, 1874." (37 & 38 Vict., cap. 77.)

The Act does not apply to the clergy of the Episcopal Church in Scotland. The legal disabilities of the Scottish clergy were removed, and their position defined, by the Act 27 & 28 Vict., cap 94.

With this exception, the Act of 1874 deals with the status of all clergy ordained by Bishops other than Bishops of Dioceses in England and Ireland. It proceeds upon the assumption that all clergymen so ordained may be admitted to exercise their functions in the Church of England; but that the Bishops of that Church have a right, in respect of these clergy, to discretionary powers, analogous to those which they have in the case of ordination.

The following are the provisions of the Act which affect the clergy ordained by Bishops other than those of (1) Dioceses in England; or (2) The Church of Ireland; or (3) The Episcopal Church in Scotland.

" Section 3.—Except as hereinafter mentioned, no person who has been or shall be ordained Priest or Deacon, as the case may be, by any Bishop other than a Bishop of a Diocese in one of the Churches aforesaid shall, unless he shall hold or have previously held preferment or a curacy in England, officiate as such Priest or Deacon in any church or chapel in England, without written permission from the Archbishop of the Province in which he proposes to officiate, and without also making and subscribing so much of the declaration contained in ' The Clerical Subscription Act, 1865,' as follows—that is to say:

"' I assent to the Thirty-nine Articles of Religion, and to the Book of Common Prayer, and of the Ordering of Bishops, Priests, and Deacons. I believe the doctrine of the Church of England as therein set forth to be agreeable to the Word of God; and in public prayer and administration of the sacraments, I, whilst ministering in England, will use the form in the said Book prescribed and none other, except so far as shall be ordered by lawful authority.'

" Section 4.—Except as hereinafter mentioned, no person who has been or shall be ordained Priest or Deacon, as the case may be, by any Bishop other than a Bishop of a Diocese in one of the Churches aforesaid, shall be entitled as such Priest or Deacon to be admitted or instituted to any benefice or other ecclesiastical preferment in England, or to act as Curate therein, without the previous consent in writing of the Bishop of the Diocese in which such preferment or curacy may be situate.

"Section 5.—Any person holding ecclesiastical preferment, or acting as Curate in any Diocese in England under the provisions of this Act, may, with the written consent of the Bishop of such Diocese, request the Archbishop of the Province to give him a licence in writing under his hand and seal in the following form—that is to say :—

"' To the Rev. *A. B.*,

"' We, *C.*, by Divine Providence Archbishop of *D.*, do hereby give you, the said *A. B.*, authority to exercise your office of Priest (*or* Deacon) according to the provisions of an Act of the thirty-seventh and thirty-eighth years of her present Majesty, intituled "An Act respecting Colonial and certain other Clergy."

"' Given under our hand and seal on the day of

"' *C.* (L.S.) *D.*' "

And if the Archbishop shall think fit to issue such licence, the same shall be registered in the registry of the Province, and the person receiving the licence shall thenceforth possess all such rights and advantages, and be subject to all such duties and liabilities, as he would have possessed and been subject to if he had been ordained by the Bishop of a Diocese in England: Provided that no such licence shall be issued to any person who has not held ecclesiastical preferment or acted as Curate for a period or periods exceeding in the aggregate two years."

The Act also contains the following provision as to the Consecration of Bishops :—

"Section 12.—It shall be lawful for the Archbishop of Canterbury or the Archbishop of York, for the time being, in consecrating any person to the office of a Bishop, for the purpose of exercising Episcopal functions elsewhere than in England, to dispense, if he think fit, with the oath of due obedience to the Archbishop."

NOTE C (page 121).

The following extract from the Report refers to this subject :—" Your Committee strongly recommend that all those Dioceses which are not as yet gathered into Provinces should, as soon as possible, form part of some Provincial organization. The particular mode of effecting this in each case must be determined by those who are concerned."

The Committee would also call attention to the concluding paragraph of the same Report :—

" In the case of the limits of an existing Province being altered, the consent of the Synod of that Province would be required for the alteration."

No. XIX. (See page 28.)

Latin and Greek Versions of the Bishops' Letter of 1878.

EPISTOLA CENTUM EPISCOPORUM

IN ANGLIA CONGREGATORUM, IN PALATIO LAMBETHANO, MENSE JULIO,

ANNO SALUTIS MDCCCLXXVIII.

Fidelibus in Christo salutem in Domino.

Nos Archiepiscopi, Metropolitani, aliique Episcopi Sanctæ Catholicæ Ecclesiæ, centum numero, cum Ecclesiâ Anglicanâ plenariè communicantes, universi super Diœceses jurisdictionem Episcopalem exercitantes, vel ad Episcopalia munia in eis obeunda legi-

K

timè delegati, multi nostrûm ex remotissimis orbis terrarum regionibus, congregati in Palatio Lambethano, anno salutis MDCCCLXXVIII. præsidente Reverendissimo Præsule Archibaldo Campbell, Divinâ Providentiâ Archiepiscopo Cantuariensi, totius Angliæ Primate, participes facti, in dicti Palatii sacello, Sacrosanctorum Mysteriorum Corporis et Sanguinis Domini Nostri Jesu Christi, et orationibus adunati ad Spiritûs Sancti directionem impetrandam, de variis præfinitis quæstionibus consilium inivimus cœtui nostro propositis, ad statum Ecclesiæ pertinentibus per diversas mundi partes diffusæ.

His quæstionibus seriò deliberandis complures dies impendimus, jamque determinationes earum a nobis approbatas fidelibus in Christo commendamus.[1]

Quæ sit optima ratio pensitantes unitatis conservandæ inter varias nostræ Communionis Ecclesias, primùm omnium Deo Omnipotenti gratias agentes quàm maximas, manifestam unitatem agnoscimus, quâ Ecclesia Anglicana, et Ecclesiæ cum illâ visibiliter communicantes, jugiter connexæ permanserunt.

Conjunctæ invicem sub Uno Divino Capite, Jesu Christo, in unius Catholicæ et Apostolicæ Ecclesiæ societate, firmiter tenentes unam Fidem, in Verbo Dei revelatam, Symbolis definitam, et a Primitivâ Ecclesiâ constanter conservatam, easdem Canonicas Scripturas Veteris et Novi Testamenti recipientes, utpote omnia continentes ad salutem sempiternam necessaria, hæ nostræ Ecclesiæ eundem Dei Sermonem prædicant, eorundem Sacramentorum, divinitus institutorum, per eorundem ordinum Apostolicorum ministerium dispensatorum, participes sunt,

---

[1] In hâc Latinâ interpretatione eorum capitulorum præcipuè delectum fecimus quæ ad Ecclesiam Universalem attinere quodammodo videbantur. In Anglico autem archetypo Relationes Delegationum (*Reports of Committees*), a Cœtu comprobatæ, plenariæ reperiuntur.

et Eundem Deum et Patrem venerantur, per Eundem Dominum Jesum Christum, in Eodem Spiritu Sancto super omnibus fidelibus effuso ad ducendos eos in omnem veritatem.

Verùm enimverò cum hâc unitate consociata nunquam non extitit ea consuetudinum, disciplinæ et rituum varietas, quæ ab illâ prærogativâ enasci solet, quam quævis Ecclesia particularis, sive nationalis, jure sibi vindicat; scilicet constituendi, immutandi, atque abrogandi cærimonias vel ritus Ecclesiasticos, humanâ tantum auctoritate ordinatos, modò omnia ad ædificationem fiant.

Libenter quidem profitemur, nullam reverà etiamnum sollicitudinis causam in hâc diversitate reperiri. Constat autem, votum aliquorum animis nuper conceptum vocibus quoque passim significatum fuisse, hoc præsertim intuitu, ut rationes quædam actu efficaces a nobis adhibeantur, ad occasiones discordiæ præcidendas, et ad illam genuinam et essentialem unitatem, quæ nostras Ecclesias indies supercrescentes complectitur, manifestandam amplius atque fovendam.

Primùm quidem hujus concordiæ tuendæ illa in mentem venit ratio, quæ inde ab Apostolis ipsis divinitùs inspiratis originem ducens, Ecclesiis omnibus in eâdem individuâ et visibili unitate continendis diu inserviit. Hodierna autem rei Christianæ ea est conditio, infausta quidem sed manifesta, ut Concilium vere Œcumenicum, ad quod Ecclesia Anglicana se paratam esse convenire semper professa est, convocari non possit. Difficultates quidem quæ impedimento sunt quominus Synodus ex omnibus Anglicanis Ecclesiis conflata congregetur, re diversæ et minus graves, nimiæ tamen nobis videntur, quàm ut illa ratio unitatis conservandæ a nobis commendetur.

Aliud autem experimentum, secundâ jam vice factum, congregatio scilicet Episcoporum ab Archiepiscopo Cantuariensi convocatorum, et Eo præsidente deliberantium, spem saltem suppeditat, quæstionem, quæ hactenus insolubilis videbatur, rerum vicissitudine divinitus ordinatâ sponte solutum iri, ita ut Procuratores Ecclesiarum, situ et administratione diversarum, consultandi invicem causâ, in unum cœtum coalescant.

Persuasum est nobis, ad unitatem in fide semel sanctis traditâ proximè accedere divini cultûs communionem, eamque societates Christianas firmissmo nexu copulare : et probè recordantes Librum Precum Communium, ab omnibus nostris Ecclesiis, aliquatenus variatum, retineri, et eximium unitatis vinculum extitisse, fratres nostros admonendos censemus, divini cultûs communionem immoderatis rituum diversitatibus in discrimen posse adduci. Intrinsecam Ecclesiarum variarum unitatem custodiendæ earum concordiæ adjumentum allaturam esse validissimum confidimus. Et dum liberè profitemur, amplam quandam rituum Ecclesiasticorum flexibilitatem esse exoptandam, quippe quæ latum quasi campum patefaciat legitimis piorum affectuum significationibus, nihilominus ad Apostolicum præceptum provocamus, " Omnia ad ædificationem fiant," et ad illam Ecclesiæ Catholicæ legem principalem, rectum ordinem commendantis atque obedientiam, etsi cum privatorum sensuum et propensionum abnegatione conjungantur, tanquam subsidia Christianæ Unitatis fundamentalia, imò etiam ad fidem ipsam efficaciter conservandam necessaria.

Nolumus huic argumento finem imponere, quin spem nostram serio testificemur, omnes Ecclesiæ fideles agnituros fore, utcunque studiis in varia inclinantes, universos oportere subjici, conscientiæ ergo, in rebus ad ritus et cærimonias attinentibus, judiciis illis auctoritatem obtinentibus, quæ ab illâ Ecclesiâ particulari vel nationali promulgata sint, sub cujus tutelâ, Dei providentiâ, sint constituti ; et sibi sedulò temperaturos ab omni qualicunque alienationis vel exacerbationis occasione; et quotidie Deum enixè obsecraturos, ut omnia Ecclesiæ membra a

Spiritu Sancto dirigantur ad quæcunque recta sint excogitanda atque exequenda ; et ut nos universi in illâ fraternâ dilectione, quæ pacis est ipsissimum vinculum et omnium virtutum, adunare dignetur.

*   *   *   *

Gratias agimus Deo Omnipotenti maximas, eò quod protestationes solennes a tot Ecclesiis et societatibus Christianis per orbem terrarum profectæ sint contra sedis Romanæ usurpationes, et contra novicia dogmata ejus auctoritate promulgata.

Affectuum benevolorum significatio debetur ab Ecclesiâ Anglicanâ universis, sive Ecclesiis, sive singulis, contra hos errores protestantibus, quippe qui difficultatibus forsitan laborent specialibus, quum propter Incredulitatis incursiones, tum vero propter Romanæ sedis arrogantiam.

Nos confitemur Unum tantum "Mediatorem Dei et hominum, Hominem Jesum Christum," "Qui est super omnia Deus in sæcula." Nos repudiamus, utpote Scripturis Sacris et Catholicæ veritati adversantem, qualemcunque doctrinam alios mediatores Ejus vice constituentem, vel aliquatenus detrahentem ab Illius Divinâ Majestate, et a plenitudine Deitatis in Illo inhabitantis, quæ immaculato illo Sacrificio, semel ab Eo in Cruce propter omnium hominum peccata oblato, infinitum pretium impertita est.

Commonendi igitur sunt a nobis fideles, facinus illud a Romano Episcopo patratum, in Concilio Vaticano, anno MDCCCLXX., quo sibi supereminentiam super omnes homines in rebus fidei et morum vindicavit, arrogatæ sibi Infallibilitatis prætextu, attributorum Ipsius Domini Nostri Jesu Christi manifestam fuisse invasionem.

Innotuerunt omnibus regulæ illæ fundamentales, juxta quas Ecclesia Anglicana seipsam reformavit. Nos Sanctas Scripturas sufficientem et supremam fidei regulam esse declaramus, et omnibus nostris diligenter scrutandas proponimus. Nos fidem nostram ipsis Symbolorum antiquorum vocibus profitemur. Nos Apostolicum ordinem Episcoporum, Presbyterorum et Diaconorum retinemus. Ecclesiarum particularium sive nationalium libertates legitimas asserimus. Nos Librum Communium Precationum, necnon Administrationis Sacramentorum, populis nostris in manus damus, vernaculo eorum sermone compositum, et juxta optima et antiquissima fidei et divini cultûs exemplaria adornatum. Orbi universo patefacta sunt hæc nostra documenta ; sciuntur et leguntur ab omnibus.

Libenter igitur amplectimur universos sese reformandi studiosos ad amussim Ecclesiæ primitivæ. Rigidam Uniformitatem non flagitamus ; supervacaneas dissensiones deprecamur. Omnibus ad nos allectis, dum jugum erroris et superstitionis excutere moliuntur, commodare operam nostrum parati sumus, et talia eis subministrare privilegia, qualia ipsis possint esse gratiosa, et nostris ipsorum institutis et formulis Ecclesiasticis consentanea.

*   *   *   *

Sed hæc hâctenus. Quod ad quæstiones attinet nobis propositas quæ leges Matrimonii tangunt, dum ex animo agnoscimus angustias, ad quas nonnullæ nostræ Ecclesiæ a popularium suorum legum lationibus redactæ sunt, censemus quoque officium esse uniuscujusque Ecclesiæ operam dare, ut sanctitati Matrimonii custodiendæ consulatur, secundum mandata in Dei Verbo præscripta. et quemadmodum ab Ecclesiâ Christi hâctenus sunt recepta.

Rixas quasdam luctuosas de rituum Ecclesiasticorum quæstionibus, considerantes, quibus nonnullæ nostræ congregationes graviter perturbatæ sunt, nos affirmamus, nihil in diu usitatâ cærimoniarum consuetudine, contra Episcopi admonitionem, debere innovari.

Denique, nonnullas novitates, quum in agendo tum in docendo, quod ad Confessionem attinet, contemplantes, nos declaramus Anglicanæ Communionis

Ecclesias firmiter eas leges tenere, quæ in hanc rem in Sacris Scripturis sunt promulgatæ, primitivæ Ecclesiæ professione sancitæ, et ab Anglicanâ Reformatione instauratæ. Et nos consultò censemus, nulli Ecclesiæ Ministro licere, ab iis, qui ad eum se recipiunt, doloris aperiendi gratiâ, omnium sigillatim peccatorum minutam enumerationem exquirere ; vel privatam confessionem iis imperare, ante Sacrosanctæ Eucharistiæ participationem ; vel præscribere, vel etiam commendare, confessionis consuetudinariæ coram sacerdote exercitationem ; vel docere talem exercitationem, vel sacerdoti subjectionem, directionis, ut aiunt, causâ, conditiones esse necessarias, ad sublimissimam vitam spiritualem attingendam. Nihilominus non in animo habemus quoquam modo terminos imponere subsidiis, quæ in Libro nostro Precum Publicarum, ad conscientiarum sollicitarum sublevationem, providè subministrantur.

Hæ sunt determinationes quæstionum nobis propositarum, quatenus Ecclesiæ Universalis vel Ecclesiarum nostrarum conditionem attingere videbantur.

Ad hæc inspicienda varias Ecclesiarum Synodos, aliosque in eis Ecclesiis auctoritatem exercitantes, et universos denique Christi fideles, per orbem terrarum invitamus. Dominationem in cleris non affectamus : sed has determinationes, a cœtu nostro approbatas, rationi et conscientiæ fratrum nostrorum, utpote a Spiritu Sancto illuminatorum, commendamus, enixè Deum apprecantes, ut omnes ubique gentium Domini Nostri Jesu Christi Nomen invocantes, unâ mente consocientur, in unâ Communione conjungantur, unam fidem semel sanctis traditam firmiter complectantur, et unum Suum Dominum in uno puritatis et dilectionis spiritu venerentur. Amen.

Subscripsi, in nomine Cœtûs Lambethani,

ARCHIBALDUS CAMPBELL,
    Archiepiscopus Cantuariensis.

ΕΠΙΣΤΟΛΗ ʽΕΚΑΤΟΝ ΕΠΙΣΚΟΠΩΝ

Ἐν Ἀγγλίᾳ συνηθροισμένων, ἐν Παλατίῳ Λαμβηθανῷ, μηνὶ Ἰουλίῳ, ἔτει ͵αωοή (1878).

Τοῖς πιστοῖς ἐν Χριστῷ Ἰησοῦ χαίρειν ἐν Κυρίῳ.

Ἡμεῖς Ἀρχιεπίσκοποι, Μητροπολῖται, καὶ ἄλλοι ἐπίσκοποι τῆς ἁγίας Καθολικῆς Ἐκκλησίας, συγκοινωνοῦντες ὁλοκλήρως τῇ Ἀγγλικανῇ Ἐκκλησίᾳ, ἑκατὸν ὄντες τὸν ἀριθμὸν, ἅπαντες ἐπισκοπὴν παροικιῶν ἐπιτηδεύοντες, ἢ νομίμως ἐπισκοπικὰ τέλη ἐν αὐταῖς ἐπιτετραμμένοι, συνελθόντες, πολλοὶ ἐξ ἡμῶν ἀπὸ τῶν μακροτάτων τῆς οἰκουμένης κλιμάτων, ἐν τῷ Παλατίῳ Λαμβηθανῷ, ἔτει τῆς τοῦ Κυρίου ἐνσαρκώσεως ͵αωοή (1878), προεδρεύοντος σεβασμιωτάτου Ἀρχιβάλδου Κάμπβελλ, τῇ θείᾳ προνοίᾳ Ἀρχιεπισκόπου Καντουαρίας, Ἐπισκόπων ὅλης Ἀγγλίας πρωτοθρόνου, μετειληφότες, ἐν τῷ ναῷ τοῦ εἰρημένου παλατίου, τῶν ἁγίων μυστηρίων τοῦ σώματος καὶ τοῦ αἵματος τοῦ Κυρίου, καὶ προσευχαῖς ἡνωμένοι ὑπὲρ τῆς τοῦ ἁγίου Πνεύματος χειραγωγίας, ἐξέτασιν πεποιήκαμεν διαφόρων ζητημάτων ἡμῖν προβεβλημένων, ἀνηκόντων εἰς τὴν τῆς Ἐκκλησίας σχέσιν ἐν διαφόροις τοῦ κόσμου μέρεσιν.

Περὶ τούτων τῶν ζητημάτων σπουδαίως διὰ πλειόνων ἡμερῶν συμβεβουλευκότες, παρατιθέμεθα τανῦν τοῖς πιστοῖς τὰ συμπεράσματα ἡμῖν ὑπὲρ αὐτῶν δεδογμένα.[1]

Ἐνθυμούμενοι τὴν ἐπιτηδειοτάτην μέθοδον πρὸς τὴν τήρησιν τῆς ἑνότητος τῶν διαφόρων τῆς ἡμετέρας κοινωνίας ἐκκλησιῶν, πρώτιστα πάντων ἀναγνωρίζομεν, μετ' ἐγκαρδίου εὐχαριστίας τῷ Παντοκράτορι Θεῷ, τὴν οὐσιώδη καὶ ἐναργῆ ἑνότητα, ἐν ᾗ ἡ Ἀγγλικανὴ Ἐκκλη-

---

[1] Ἐν ταύτῃ τῇ μεταφράσει, τῶν κεφαλαίων ἐκλογὴν πεποιήκαμεν, τῶν μάλιστα τῇ καθόλου Ἐκκλησίᾳ προσηκόντων· ἐν δὲ τῷ Ἀγγλικῷ τῆς Ἐπιστολῆς ἀρχετύπῳ αἱ τῶν ἐπιτρόπων τοῦ συμβουλίου ἐκθέσεις (*Reports of Committees*), ἀπὸ τοῦ Συμβουλίου δοκιμασθεῖσαι, ὁλοτελεῖς εὑρίσκονται.

σία, καὶ αἱ ἐκκλησίαι μετ' αὐτῆς ὁρατῶς συγκοινωνοῦσαι, διατελοῦσι συνημμέναι. Ἡνωμέναι ὑπὸ μιᾶς θείας Κεφαλῆς, Ἰησοῦ Χριστοῦ, ἐν τῇ κοινωνίᾳ τῆς μιᾶς Καθολικῆς Ἐκκλησίας, κατέχουσαι τὴν μίαν πίστιν, ἐν ταῖς ἁγίαις Γραφαῖς ἀποκεκαλυμμένην, ἐν τοῖς Συμβόλοις ὡρισμένην, καὶ ὑπὸ τῆς ἀρχῆθεν Ἐκκλησίας κεκρατημένην, δεχόμεναι τὰς αὐτὰς κανονικὰς Γραφὰς τῆς παλαιᾶς καὶ τῆς καινῆς Διαθήκης, ὡς τὰ πάντα πρὸς σωτηρίαν ἀναγκαῖα περιεχούσας, αὗται αἱ ἡμέτεραι Ἐκκλησίαι τὸν αὐτὸν τοῦ Θεοῦ λόγον κηρύσσουσι, τῶν αὐτῶν θεόθεν διατεταγμένων μυστηρίων μεταλαμβάνουσι διὰ τῆς ὑπηρεσίας τῶν αὐτῶν ἀποστολικῶν βαθμῶν, καὶ προσκυνοῦσι τῷ αὐτῷ Θεῷ καὶ Πατέρι, διὰ τοῦ αὐτοῦ Κυρίου Ἰησοῦ Χριστοῦ, ἐν τῷ αὐτῷ ἁγίῳ καὶ θείῳ Πνεύματι, πᾶσι τοῖς πιστεύουσιν ἐπιχορηγουμένῳ, πρὸς τὸ ὁδηγεῖν αὐτοὺς εἰς πᾶσαν τὴν ἀλήθειαν.

Ἀμέσως μὲν οὖν μετὰ ταύτης τῆς ἑνότητος, ὑπῆρξεν ἐν ἡμετέραις ἐκκλησίαις ἐκείνη συνηθείας, διατάξεως, καὶ λειτουργίας διαφορά, ἥτις ἀναγκαίως ἐκφύεται ἐξ ἀσκήσεως τῆς ἐξουσίας, τῆς ἑκάστῃ μερικῇ ἢ ἐθνικῇ ἐκκλησίᾳ προσηκούσης, τοῦ διατάσσειν, παραχαράσσειν, καὶ ἀκυροῦν θεσμοὺς καὶ τελετὰς ἐκκλησιαστικάς, ὑπ' ἀνθρωπίνης ἐξουσίας διατεταγμένας, μόνον ὥστε πάντα πρὸς οἰκοδομὴν γίγνεσθαι.

Ἀσμένως μὲν ὁμολογοῦμεν μηδεμίαν εἰσέτι εὑρίσκεσθαι μερίμνης αἰτίαν, διὰ ταύτην τὴν διαφωνίαν. Ὅμως μέντοι ἐπιπόθησίς τις νεωστὶ ἐπιπολὺ αἰσθήσει καὶ λόγῳ πεφανέρωται, ὡς ἐννοητέα καὶ προσαπτέα εἴη ὄργανά τινα, πρὸς τὸ ἐκκόπτειν, εἰ τύχοι, ἀφορμὰς διχοστασίας, καὶ πρὸς τὴν λαμπροτέραν ἀπόδειξιν καὶ αὔξησιν τῆς ἀληθινῆς καὶ οὐσιώδους ὁμονοίας ἐν ἡμετέραις ἐκκλησίαις ὑπαρχούσης.

Τὸ πρῶτον μὲν εἰς νοῦν ἀνερχόμενον ὄργανον τοιαύτης ἑνώσεως εὐλόγως ἂν εἴη ἐκεῖνο, ὅπερ, ἀρχὴν ἔχον ἀπὸ τῶν θεοφόρων ἀποστόλων, συνέζευξεν ἁπάσας τὰς Χριστοῦ ἐκκλησίας ἐν μιᾷ ἀδιαιρέτῳ καὶ ὁρατῇ κοινωνίᾳ. Ἀλλὰ μὲν οὖν ἡ συνάθροισις ἀληθινῶς οἰκουμενικῆς Συνόδου, πρὸς ὁποίαν ἡ Ἀγγλικανὴ Ἐκκλησία πάντοτε ἐπηγγέλλετο ἑτοίμη εἶναι συνέρχεσθαι, ἐν τῇ σημερινῇ τοῦ Χριστιανισμοῦ καταστάσει, δυστυχῶς μὲν, ἄλλα φανερῶς, πέφυκεν ἀμήχανος. Αἱ μὲν ἀπορίαι, αἵτινες παρακολουθήσειαν ἂν τῇ συνελεύσει συνόδου ἐκ πασῶν τῶν ἀγγλικανῶν ἐκκλησιῶν συγκεκροτημένης, καίπερ ἀνόμοιοι καὶ μετριώτεραι τῶν εἰρημένων, ὅμως μέντοι εἰσὶ βαρύτεραι ἢ συγχωρῆσαι ταύτης τῆς μεθόδου, ἐν τῷ νῦν χρόνῳ, συναίνεσιν. Ἀλλ' ἡ πεῖρα, δὶς γεγονυῖα, συμβουλίου ἐπισκόπων, ἀπὸ τοῦ Καντουαρίας Ἀρχιεπισκόπου συγκεκλημένων, καὶ ὑπ' αὐτοῦ προεδρεύοντος συνηθροισμένων, ἐλπίδα ἡμῖν παρέχει αὐτομάτου λύσεως προβλήματος μέχρι τοῦ νῦν ἀλύτου, δηλονότι συναθροίσεως καὶ συμβουλεύσεως τοποτηρητῶν ἐκκλησιῶν τῇ τε θέσει καὶ τῇ διοικήσει διαφερουσῶν.

Ἐγγύτατα μετὰ τὴν ἑνότητα ἐν τῇ πίστει, τῇ τοῖς ἁγίοις ἅπαξ παραδοθείσῃ, πεπεισμένοι ἐσμὲν τὴν θρησκείας κοινωνίαν ἰσχυρότατον εἶναι σύνδεσμον πρὸς τὴν σύναψιν τῶν χριστιανικῶν ἑταιριῶν· καὶ καλῶς μεμνημένοι ὅτι τὸ ἡμέτερον τῶν δημοσίων προσευχῶν βιβλίον, μετά τινων οἵων δήποτε ἀλλοιώσεων ἐν πάσαις ἡμετέραις ἐκκλησίαις κατεχόμενον, ἐξαίρετόν τι ἑνότητος γέγονε φυλακτήριον, νουθετεῖν ἀξιοῦμεν τοὺς ἡμεδαποὺς, ὅτι αὕτη ἡ θρησκείας κοινωνία κινδυνεύοι ἂν λυμαίνεσθαι δι' ὑπερβολικῶν ἱερουργίας παραλλάξεων. Ἡ ἐσωτερικὴ μὲν τῶν ἐκκλησιῶν ἑνότης ταύτῃ τῇ θρησκείας κοινωνίᾳ, καθὼς πεποίθαμεν, ὑπηρετήσει· ἀλλ' ὅμως, (καίπερ ἐννοοῦντες ὅτι τοία τις ἀμφιλαφὴς λειτουργικῶν τελετῶν ἐλευθερία αἱρετή ἐστιν, οἵα πάσαις ταῖς νομίμαις θρησκευτικῶν αἰσθημάτων ἀποδείξεσιν εὐρυχωρίαν ἂν χαρίσαιτο,) τὴν ἀποστολικὴν παραγγελίαν ἐπικαλούμεθα, "πάντα πρὸς οἰκοδομὴν γιγνέσθω," καὶ τὸν καθολικὸν κανόνα ἐπιμαρτυρόμεθα, τὸν διορίζοντα εὐταξίαν καὶ πειθαρχίαν, καίπερ μετ' αὐταπαρνήσεως ἰδίων προσκλίσεων καὶ αἰσθήσεων ἀποδιδομένας, ὡς χριστιανικῆς ἑνότητος θεμέλια, καὶ ὡς ἀναγκαίας πρὸς αὐτῆς τῆς πίστεως νικηφόρον ὑπεράσπισιν. Τοιγαροῦν οὐ παυσόμεθα τοιαῦτα νουθετοῦντες πρὶν ἐκφωνῆσαι ἐκτενῶς τὴν ἐλπίδα, ὅτι πάντα τῶν ἡμετέρων ἐκκλησιῶν τέκνα, ὁποίαις τισὶν οὖν θεωρίαις διαφέροντα, μέλλουσιν ὁμολογεῖν τὸ καθῆκον τοῦ ὑποτάσσεσθαι, διὰ τὴν συνείδησιν, ἐν θεσμοῖς καὶ τελεταῖς θρησκευτικαῖς, ταῖς ἐξουσιαστικαῖς κρίσεσιν τῆς μερικῆς ἢ ἐθνικῆς ἐκκλησίας, ὑφ' ἧς θείᾳ προνοίᾳ τυγχάνωσι κατῳκισμένα· καὶ ὅτι ἀφέξονται παντὸς πράγματος εἰς ἀλλοτρίωσιν ἢ ἐρεθισμὸν τείνοντος, καὶ ὁσήμερον θερμῶς προσεύξονται, ἵνα τὸ ἅγιον Πνεῦμα πάντα τῆς ἐκκλησίας μέλη ὁδηγῇ εἰς τὸ λογίζεσθαι καὶ ἐργάζεσθαι πάντοτε ἃ δεῖ, καὶ ἡμᾶς πάντας συνάπτῃ τῇ φιλαδελφικῇ ἐκείνῃ ἀγάπῃ, ἥτις ἐστὶν αὐτὸς εἰρήνης καὶ πασῶν ἀρετῶν σύνδεσμος.

* * * *

Εὐχαριστοῦμεν τῷ Παντοκράτορι Θεῷ, ὅτι σεμνοπρεπής τις διαμαρτυρία ἐξήχηται ἀπὸ πάνυ πολλῶν ἐκκλησιῶν, καὶ ἀπὸ κοινοτήτων χριστιανῶν καθ' ὅλον τὸν κόσμον, κατὰ τῶν τῆς Ῥωμαίας καθέδρας πλεονεκτημάτων, καὶ κατὰ τῶν νεωτερικῶν δογμάτων, ὑπ' ἐξουσίας αὐτῆς διωρισμένων.

Ἡ Ἀγγλικανὴ Ἐκκλησία ὀφείλει πᾶσαν συμπάθειαν ἐκκλησίαις κοινῇ, καὶ χριστιανοῖς ἰδίᾳ, διαμαρτυρομένοις κατὰ τούτων πλανημάτων, καὶ στενοχωρουμένοις, εἰ τύχοι, ὑπ' ἀποριῶν ἐξάλλων, διὰ τῶν τῆς ἀπιστίας προσβολῶν, ἅμα καὶ διὰ τῶν τῆς Ῥώμης ἐπιχειρημάτων.

Ἡμεῖς ὁμολογοῦμεν ἕνα μόνον Μεσίτην θεοῦ καὶ ἀνθρώπων, Ἄνθρωπον Ἰησοῦν Χριστόν, ὅς ἐστιν ἐπὶ πάντων Θεὸς εὐλογητὸς εἰς τοὺς αἰῶνας. Ἀπωθούμεθα, ὡς ἐναντίον ταῖς Γραφαῖς καὶ τῇ καθολικῇ ἀληθείᾳ, πᾶν ὁτιοῦν δόγμα, ὅπερ καθιστάναι ἄλλους μεσίτας ἀντ' Ἐκείνου τολμήσειεν ἄν, ἢ ἀφαιρεῖν ὁτιοῦν ἀπὸ τῆς θείας μεγαλειότητος τοῦ πληρώματος τῆς θεότητος ἐν Αὐτῷ κατοικοῦντος, καὶ τιμὴν ἄπειρον παρέχοντος τῇ ἀμώμῳ ἐκείνῃ θυσίᾳ, τῇ ἅπαξ ὑπ' Αὐτοῦ ὑπὲρ τοῦ ὅλου τοῦ κόσμου ἁμαρτιῶν ἐπὶ σταυροῦ προσενεχθείσης.

Χρεωστοῦμεν οὖν νουθετεῖν τοὺς πιστούς, τὸ ἔργον ὃ κατείργασται ὁ τῆς Ῥώμης ἐπίσκοπος ἔτει 1870 ἐν τῇ Βατικανῇ συνόδῳ, δι' οὗ ὑπεροχῆς ἀντεποιήσατο ὑπὲρ πάντων ἀνθρώπων, τήν τε πίστιν καὶ τὰ ἤθη, ἐπὶ προσχήματι ἀπλανησίας ἑαυτῷ ἐφαρπασθείσης, ἐπέμβασιν γεγονέναι τῶν ἀξιωμάτων τῷ Κυρίῳ Ἰησοῦ Χριστῷ προσηκόντων.

Γνώριμοι πᾶσίν εἰσιν οἱ κανόνες, καθ' οὓς ἡ Ἀγγλικανὴ Ἐκκλησία ἑαυτὴν μετερρύθμισεν. Ἀνακηρύττομεν τὴν αὐτάρκειαν καὶ τὴν ὑπεροχὴν τῶν ἱερῶν Γραφῶν, ὡς ὁριστικὴν πίστεως στάθμην, καὶ τῷ ἡμετέρῳ λαῷ παραγγέλλομεν σπουδαίαν αὐτῶν μελέτην· τὴν πίστιν ἡμῶν ταῖς τῶν ἀρχαίων Συμβόλων φωναῖς ὁμολογοῦμεν· τὸ ἀποστολικὸν τάγμα Ἐπισκόπων, Πρεσβυτέρων καὶ Διακόνων κατέχομεν· τὴν ἔννομον ἐλευθερίαν μερικῶν ἢ ἐθνικῶν ἐκκλησιῶν διαβεβαιούμεθα· τῷ λαῷ ἡμῶν ἐγχειρίζομεν, ἐν τῇ ἐγχωρίῳ αὐτοῦ διαλέκτῳ, βιβλίον προσευχῶν δημοσίων καὶ τελετῶν, καὶ τῶν μυστηρίων ἱερουργίας, κατὰ τὰ ἄριστα καὶ παλαιότατα χριστιανικῆς πίστεως καὶ λατρείας ἀρχέτυπα.

Ταῦτα τὰ ἡμῶν μαρτυρήματα ἐνώπιον τῆς οἰκουμένης ἀναπτύσσεται, γιγνωσκόμενα καὶ ἀναγιγνωσκόμενα ὑπὸ πάντων ἀνθρώπων.

Ἀσμένως οὖν ἀσπαζόμεθα πᾶσαν πεῖραν μεταρρυθμίσεως κατὰ τὸ παράδειγμα τῆς ἀρχαίας ἐκκλησίας· στερεὰν ταυτότητα οὐκ ἀπαιτοῦμεν· ἀνωφελεῖς διχοστασίας παραιτούμεθα· πᾶσιν τοῖς πρὸς ἡμᾶς ἐφελκομένοις ἐν τῷ ἐπιχειρεῖν ἑαυτοὺς ἐλευθερῶσαι ἀπὸ ζυγοῦ πλάνης καὶ δεισιδαιμονίας πᾶσαν βοήθειαν προθύμως προτείνομεν, καὶ οἷα ἑαυτοῖς προνόμια εἴη ἀρεστά, καὶ ἡμετέροις κανόσιν, τοῖς ἐν ἡμετέραις διατυπώσεσιν ὡρισμένοις, σύμφωνα, ἐθελόντως προκομίζομεν.

*   *   *   *

Περὶ τῶν ζητημάτων ἡμῖν παρατεθέντων ὑπὲρ τῶν τοῦ Γάμου νόμων ἐμφανίζομεν, ὅτι τὰς ἀπορίας ἐπιγιγνώσκοντες, ἐν αἷς ἔνιαι ἐκκλησίαι ἐμπλέκονται, διὰ τῶν θεσμῶν τῆς τοπικῆς νομοθεσίας, νομίζομεν ὅτι δεῖ πᾶσαν ἐκκλησίαν, κατὰ τὴν ἑαυτῆς γνώμην, τὴν τοῦ Γάμου ἁγιωσύνην διαφυλάττειν, κατὰ τὰ ἐν τῷ ῥήματι τοῦ Θεοῦ ὁρισθέντα, καὶ καθὰ ἡ τοῦ Χριστοῦ Ἐκκλησία μέχρι τοῦ νῦν ταῦτα δέδεκται.

Ἀναθεωροῦντες τοὺς λυγροὺς διαλογισμούς, περὶ τελετῶν ἐκκλησιαστικῶν, δι' ὧν ἔνια τῶν ἡμετέρων πλήθη χαλεπῶς τεθορύβηνται, διαβεβαιούμεθα τὸν κανόνα, ὁρίζοντα μηδὲν δεῖν νεωτερίζειν, ἐν τῇ εἰθισμένῃ θρησκείας διατάξει, κατὰ τῆς τοῦ ἐπισκόπου νουθεσίας.

Λοιπὸν ἐνθυμούμενοι καινοτομίας τινὰς, τῇ τε πράξει καὶ τῇ διδαχῇ, περὶ τῆς ἐξομολογήσεως, διϊσχυριζόμεθα, τὰς τῆς Ἀγγλικανῆς κοινωνίας Ἐκκλησίας κρατεῖν βεβαίως τοὺς κανόνας περὶ τῆς ἐξομολογήσεως ἐν ταῖς ἁγίαις Γραφαῖς ἀποδεδειγμένους, καὶ ὑπὸ τῆς ἀρχαίας Ἐκκλησίας συνωμολογημένους, καὶ ἐν τῇ Ἀγγλικῇ Μεταρρυθμίσει ἀνακεκαινωμένους· καὶ ἐσκεμμένως ἐγνώκαμεν, μηδενὶ τῆς ἐκκλησίας ὑπηρέτῃ ἐξεῖναι ἀπαιτεῖν ἐκ τῶν πρὸς αὐτὸν φοιτώντων, διὰ τὴν τῆς αὐτῶν λύπης ἀνάπτυξιν, ἁπασῶν τῶν ἁμαρτιῶν κατὰ μέρος ἑκάστων ἐξαρίθμησιν, ἢ ἰδίαν ἐξομολόγησιν ἐκβασανίζειν, πρὸ τῆς ἁγίας εὐχαριστίας μεταλήψεως, ἢ ἐπιτάσσειν ἢ καὶ παραινεῖν τὴν τῆς συνήθους τῷ ἱερεῖ ἐξομολογήσεως ἐπιτήδευσιν, ἢ διδάσκειν ὅτι τοία ἐπιτήδευσις, ἢ τὸ ὑποτάσσεσθαι τῇ οὑτωσὶ καλουμένῃ ἱερέως χειραγωγίᾳ, ἀναγκαῖά ἐστι προπαιδεύματα πρὸς τὴν τῆς ἀνωτάτης πνευματικῆς ζωῆς ἐπίβασιν. Ὅμως μέντοι οὐδαμῶς ἐννοοῦμεν ἐπιτέμνειν τὴν ἐν τῇ βίβλῳ τῶν δημοσίων προσευχῶν, πρὸς τὸν βεβαρημένων συνειδήσεων ἐπικουφισμὸν, ἐπιχορηγίαν προνενοημένην.

Ταῦτά ἐστι τὰ συμπεράσματα εἰς ἃ κατηντήκαμεν, περὶ τῶν ἡμῖν προβεβλημένων ζητημάτων, ἐν οἷς τὰ πάντων τῆς Καθολικῆς Ἐκκλησίας τέκνων ἁπτόμενα ταῖς συνόδοις ἐκκλησιῶν, καὶ ταῖς ἐξουσίαις καθ' ἑκάστην κυβερνητικαῖς, καὶ πᾶσιν ἁπλῶς τοῖς πιστοῖς ἐν Χριστῷ Ἰησοῦ φιλοφρόνως σαφηνίζομεν.

Οὐκ ἀντιποιούμεθα τοῦ κατακυριεύειν ἐν κλήροις, ἀλλὰ ταῦτα τῷ ἡμετέρῳ συμβουλίῳ ἀρέσαντα συνίσταμεν τῷ λογισμῷ καὶ τῇ συνειδήσει τῶν ἀδελφῶν, ὡς ὑπὸ τοῦ ἁγίου Πνεύματος πεφωτισμένων, ἐκτενῶς Θεῷ προσευχόμενοι, ἵνα πάντες οἱ τὸ ὄνομα τοῦ Κυρίου ἐπικαλούμενοι, μιᾷ γνώμῃ καὶ μιᾷ κοινωνίᾳ ἡνωμένοι, τὴν πίστιν τὴν ἅπαξ τοῖς ἁγίοις παραδοθεῖσαν βεβαίως κρατῶσιν, καὶ τῷ ἑνὶ αὐτῶν Κυρίῳ ἐν ἑνὶ ἀφθαρσίας καὶ ἀγάπης πνεύματι λατρεύωσιν. Ἀμήν.

Ὑπέγραψα ἐν τῷ ὀνόματι τοῦ συμβουλίου,

ΑΡΧΙΒΑΛΔΟΣ ΚΑΜΠΒΕΛΛ,
Ὁ Καντουαρίας Ἀρχιεπίσκοπος.

No. XX. (See page 30.)

Official List of the Bishops present at the Lambeth Conference of 1878.

The Archbishop of Canterbury.
The Archbishop of York.
The Archbishop of Armagh.
The Archbishop of Dublin.

The Bishop of London.
The Bishop of Winchester.
The Bishop of Llandaff.
The Bishop of Ripon.
The Bishop of Norwich.
The Bishop of Bangor.
The Bishop of Gloucester and Bristol.
The Bishop of Chester.
The Bishop of St. Alban's.
The Bishop of Hereford.
The Bishop of Peterborough.
The Bishop of Lincoln.
The Bishop of Salisbury.
The Bishop of Carlisle.
The Bishop of Exeter.
The Bishop of Bath and Wells.
The Bishop of Oxford.
The Bishop of Manchester.
The Bishop of Chichester.
The Bishop of St. Asaph.
The Bishop of Ely.
The Bishop of St. David's.
The Bishop of Truro.
The Bishop of Rochester.
The Bishop of Lichfield.
The Bishop of Sodor and Man.

The Bishop of Meath.
The Bishop of Down.
The Bishop of Killaloe.
The Bishop of Limerick.
The Bishop of Derry.
The Bishop of Cashel.
The Bishop of Ossory.

The Bishop of Moray. Primus.
The Bishop of St. Andrew's.

The Bishop of Edinburgh.
The Bishop of Aberdeen.
The Bishop of Glasgow.
The Bishop of Brechin.
The Bishop of Argyll.

The Bishop of Delaware.
The Bishop of New York.
The Bishop of Ohio.
The Bishop of Pennsylvania.
The Bishop of Western New York.
The Bishop of Nebraska.
The Bishop of Pittsburgh.
The Bishop of Louisiana.
The Bishop of Missouri.
The Bishop of Long Island.
The Bishop of Albany.
The Bishop of Central Pennsylvania.
The Assistant Bishop of North Carolina.
The Bishop of New Jersey.
The Bishop of Wisconsin.
The Bishop of Iowa.
The Bishop of Colorado.

The Bishop of Haiti.
The Bishop of Shanghai.

The Bishop of Montreal. Metropolitan.
The Bishop of Fredericton.
The Bishop of Nova Scotia.
The Bishop of Ontario.
The Bishop of Huron.
The Bishop of Toronto.
The Bishop of Niagara.

The Bishop of Madras.
The Bishop of Colombo.
The Bishop of Bombay.

Official List of Bishops Present, 1878.

The Bishop of Guiana.
The Bishop of Kingston.
The Bishop of Antigua.
The Bishop of Barbados.
The Bishop of Nassau.

The Bishop of Sydney. Metropolitan.
The Bishop of Adelaide.
The Bishop of North Queensland.

The Bishop of Christchurch. Metropolitan.
The Bishop of Dunedin.

The Bishop of Gibraltar.

The Bishop of Capetown. Metropolitan.
The Bishop of St. Helena.
The Bishop of Maritzburgh.

The Bishop of Bloemfontein.
The Bishop of Pretoria.

The Bishop of Rupertsland. Metropolitan.
The Bishop of British Columbia.
The Bishop of Saskatchewan.

The Bishop of the Falkland Islands.

The Bishop Suffragan of Dover.
The Bishop Suffragan of Guildford.
The Bishop Suffragan of Nottingham.

Bishop Perry.
Bishop McDougall.
Bishop Ryan.
Bishop Claughton.

OFFICERS OF THE CONFERENCE.

THE BISHOP OF GLOUCESTER & BRISTOL,
Secretary of the Conference.

THE BISHOP OF EDINBURGH,
Secretary of Committees.

ISAMBARD BRUNEL, D.C.L.,
Chancellor of the Diocese of Ely,
} *Assistant Secretary.*

No. XXI. (See page 25.)

Order of Bishops in the Processions at Lambeth Palace and in St. Paul's Cathedral in 1878.

The following is an official list, as prepared for the Processions on July 2 and July 27, 1878. The order had to be materially changed on the occasion of the actual services, by the absence, at the moment, of

Bishops who had been expected, but the same principle of arrangement was in each case followed. The Archbishop of Canterbury had the Archbishop of York and the Bishop of London on his right and left hand, and was preceded by the Metropolitans of the Irish, Scottish, and Colonial Provinces. The Bishops from the United States walked, as guests, abreast of the English Diocesans. The other Bishops were arranged, two and two, according to date of consecration. The processions moved, as usual, in reverse order, the junior Bishops first, the Archbishops last.

Archbishop of York.	Archbishop of Canterbury.	Bishop of London.
	,, Armagh.	
	,, Dublin.	
Bishop of Delaware.	Primus of Scottish Episcopal Church.	,, Winchester.
,, New York.	Bishop of Sydney.	,, Llandaff.
,, Ohio.	,, Christchurch, New Zealand.	,, Ripon.
,, Pennsylvania.	,, Montreal.	,, Bangor.
,, Western New York.	,, Capetown.	,, { Gloucester & Bristol.
,, Nebraska.	,, Rupert's Land.	,, Chester.
Bishop of Pittsburgh.		Bishop of St. Alban's.
,, Louisiana.		,, Hereford.
,, Missouri.		,, Peterborough.
,, Long Island.		,, Lincoln.
,, Albany.		,, Salisbury.
,, Central Pennsylvania.		,, Carlisle.
Assistant Bishop of North Carolina.		,, Exeter.
Bishop of New Jersey.		,, Bath and Wells.
,, Wisconsin.		,, Oxford.
,, Iowa.		,, Manchester.
,, Colorada.		,, Chichester.
,, St. Asaph.		,, Ely.
,, St. David's.		,, Rochester.
,, Truro.		,, Lichfield.
,, Sodor and Man.		,, Dover.
,, Guildford.		,, Nottingham.
Bishop Perry.		,, Killaloe.
,, M'Dougall.		Bishop Ryan.
Bishop of Meath.		,, Claughton.

And the other Bishops according to their date of consecration.

No. XXII. (See page 31.)

Invitations to the Conference of 1888.

[Although the foregoing pages have dealt only with the Conferences of 1867 and 1878, it may be of interest to append copies of the circular letters of invitation issued in 1886 and 1887 in connexion with the Conference now about to assemble in July, 1888.]

LAMBETH PALACE, *July*, 1886.

RIGHT REVEREND AND DEAR BROTHER,

There appears to be a general desire that a Conference of the Bishops of the Anglican Communion should again be held at Lambeth within the next few years.

I have accordingly decided (following the precedents of 1867 and 1878) to issue next year an invitation to such a Conference, which would assemble, according to our present plan, in the summer of 1888.

It will be of material assistance to myself and to those who are good enough to co-operate with me in making the necessary arrangements, if you can, at your early convenience, inform me whether it seems to you probable that you will be able to take part in our deliberations, and whether there are any subjects of general importance which appear to you specially appropriate for discussion in the Conference.

I am in hopes that the suggestions which may reach me in answer to this circular letter will enable me to issue, next spring, the formal invitations to the Conference, together with an intimation as to the definite subjects which will, in the following year, come before us for discussion.

I have made these preliminary arrangements in

conjunction with the Archbishop of York and the English Bishops, and I am glad to be able to inform you that the Bishop of Gloucester and Bristol, whose efficient aid as hon. Episcopal Secretary both in 1867 and 1878 will be gratefully remembered, has again kindly consented to act in that capacity. We have associated with him as Hon. Assistant Secretary the Dean of Windsor, who, as resident chaplain to Archbishop Tait, was responsible for many of the arrangements of the Conference of 1878.

It is not necessary that I should assure you of our earnest desire that you will unite with us in humble prayer to Almighty God that His guidance and blessing may be vouchsafed in rich measure, both to our ultimate deliberations and to the arrangements necessary to secure their efficiency.

I remain,
Your faithful Brother and Servant in Christ,

EDW. CANTUAR.

The Right Reverend the Bishop of

LAMBETH PALACE, *9th November*, 1887.

RIGHT REVEREND AND DEAR BROTHER,

I am now able to send you definite information with regard to the Conference of Bishops of the Anglican Communion to be held at Lambeth, if God permit, in the summer of next year.

In accordance with the precedent of 1878, it has been arranged that the Conference shall assemble on Tuesday, July 3rd, 1888. After four days' session there will be an adjournment, in order that the various Committees appointed by the Conference may have opportunity of deliberation. The Conference will re-assemble on Monday, July 23rd, or Tuesday, July 24th, and will conclude its session on Friday, July 27th.

Information as to the Services to be held in connexion with the Conference, and other particulars, will be made public as the time draws near.

I have received valuable suggestions from my Episcopal brethren in all parts of the world as to the subjects upon which it is thought desirable that we should deliberate.

These suggestions have been carefully weighed by myself and by the Bishops who have been good enough to co-operate with me in making the preliminary arrangements, and the following are the subjects definitely selected for discussion :—

I. The Church's practical work in relation to (A) Intemperance, (B) Purity, (C) Care of Emigrants, (D) Socialism.
II. Definite Teaching of the Faith to various classes, and the means thereto.
III. The Anglican Communion in relation to the Eastern Churches, to the Scandinavian and other Reformed Churches, to the Old Catholics, and others.
IV. Polygamy of heathen converts. Divorce.
V. Authoritative standards of Doctrine and Worship.
VI. Mutual relations of Dioceses and Branches of the Anglican Communion.

May I venture again to invite your earnest prayer that the Divine Head of the Church may be pleased to prosper with His blessing this our endeavour to promote His glory, and the advancement of His Kingdom upon earth?

I remain,
Your faithful Brother and Servant in Christ,
EDW. CANTUAR.

The Right Reverend the Bishop of

WYMAN AND SONS, PRINTERS, GREAT QUEEN STREET, LONDON, W.C.

Society for Promoting Christian Knowledge.

Publications on
THE CHRISTIAN EVIDENCE.

BOOKS.

	Price.
	s. d.
Christianity Judged by its Fruits. By the Rev. C. Croslegh, D.D. Post 8vo ......*Cloth boards*	1 6
The Great Passion-Prophecy Vindicated. By the Rev. Brownlow Maitland, M.A. Post 8vo. *Limp cloth*	0 10
Natural Theology of Natural Beauty (The). By the Rev. R. St. John Tyrwhitt, M.A. Post 8vo. *Cloth boards*	1 6
Steps to Faith. Addresses on some points in the Controversy with Unbelief. By the Rev. Brownlow Maitland, M.A. Post 8vo. *Cloth boards*	1 6
Scepticism and Faith. By the Rev. Brownlow Maitland. Post 8vo. *Cloth boards*	1 4
Theism or Agnosticism. An Essay on the grounds of Belief in God. By the Rev. Brownlow Maitland, M.A. Post 8vo............*Cloth boards*	1 6
Argument from Prophecy (The). By the Rev. Brownlow Maitland, M.A., Author of "Scepticism and Faith," &c. Post 8vo. ....*Cloth boards*	1 6
Some Modern Religious Difficulties. Six Sermons preached, by the request of the Christian Evidence Society, at St. James's, Piccadilly, in 1876; with a Preface by his Grace the late Archbishop of Canterbury. Post 8vo. ....*Cloth boards*	1 6
Some Witnesses for the Faith. Six Sermons preached, by the request of the Christian Evidence Society, at St. Stephen's Church, South Kensington, in 1877. Post 8vo. ....*Cloth boards*	1 4
Theism and Christianity. Six Sermons preached, by the request of the Christian Evidence Society, at St. James's, Piccadilly, in 1878. Post 8vo. ....*Cloth boards*	1 6

1-10-85.]

Publications on the Christian Evidence.

                                                                        Price.
                                                                         s. d.

Being of God, Six Addresses on the.
By C. J. Ellicott, D.D., Bishop of Gloucester and Bristol.
Small Post 8vo. .... *Cloth boards* 1 6

Modern Unbelief: its Principles and Charac-
TERISTICS. By the Right Rev. the Lord Bishop of Gloucester
and Bristol. Post 8vo. .... *Cloth boards* 1 6

When was the Pentateuch Written?
By George Warington, B.A., Author of "Can we Believe
in Miracles?" &c. Post 8vo........................ *Cloth boards* 1 6

The Analogy of Religion.
Dialogues founded upon Butler's "Analogy of Religion."
By the late Rev. H. R. Huckin, D.D., Head Master of
Repton School. Post 8vo. .... *Cloth boards* 3 0

"Miracles."
By the Rev. E. A. Litton, M.A., Examining Chaplain of
the Bishop of Durham. Crown 8vo. .... *Cloth boards* 1 6

Moral Difficulties connected with the Bible.
Being the Boyle Lectures for 1871. By the Ven. Arch-
deacon Hessey, D.C.L., Preacher to the Hon. Society of
Gray's Inn, &c. FIRST SERIES. Post 8vo. ...*Cloth boards* 1 6

Moral Difficulties connected with the Bible.
Being the Boyle Lectures for 1872. By the Ven. Arch-
deacon Hessey, D.C.L. SECOND SERIES. Post 8vo.
Cloth boards 2 6

Prayer and recent Difficulties about it.
The Boyle Lectures for 1873, being the THIRD SERIES
of "Moral Difficulties connected with the Bible."
By the Ven. Archdeacon Hessey, D.C.L. Post 8vo.
Cloth boards 2 6
The above Three Series in a volume .... *Cloth boards* 6 0

Historical Illustrations of the Old Testament.
By the Rev. G. Rawlinson, M.A., Camden Professor of
Ancient History, Oxford. Post 8vo .... *Cloth boards* 1 6

Can we Believe in Miracles?
By G. Warington, B.A., of Caius College, Cambridge.
Post 8vo... *Cloth boards* 1 6

The Moral Teaching of the New Testament
VIEWED AS EVIDENTIAL TO ITS HISTORICAL TRUTH. By the
Rev. C. A. Row, M.A. Post 8vo.................. *Cloth boards* 1 9

Scripture Doctrine of Creation.
By the Rev. T. R. Birks, M.A., Professor of Moral Philosophy
at Cambridge. Post 8vo............................ *Cloth boards* 1 6

| | Price. |
| | s. d. |

The Witness of the Heart to Christ.
Being the Hulsean Lectures for 1878. By the Right Rev. **W. Boyd Carpenter**, Bishop of Ripon. Post 8vo. *Cl. boards* ... 1 6

Thoughts on the First Principles of the Positive
PHILOSOPHY, CONSIDERED IN RELATION TO THE HUMAN MIND. By the late Benjamin Shaw, M.A., late Fellow of Trinity College, Camb. Post 8vo. ....*Limp cloth* 0 8

Thoughts on the Bible.
By the late Rev. W. Gresley, M.A., Prebendary of Lichfield. Post 8vo. ....*Cloth boards* 1 6

The Reasonableness of Prayer.
By the Rev. P. Onslow, M.A. Post 8vo. ....*Paper cover* 0 8

Paley's Evidences of Christianity.
A New Edition, with Notes, Appendix, and Preface. By the Rev. E. A. Litton, M.A. Post 8vo.......... *Cloth boards* 4 0

Paley's Natural Theology.
Revised to harmonize with Modern Science. By Mr. F. le Gros Clark, F.R.S., President of the Royal College of Surgeons of England, &c. Post 8vo. ....*Cloth boards* 4 0

Paley's Horæ Paulinæ.
A new Edition, with Notes, Appendix, and Preface. By J. S. Howson, D.D., Dean of Chester. Post 8vo. *Cloth boards* 3 0

Religion and Morality
By the Rev. Richard T. Smith, B.D., Canon of St. Patrick's, Dublin. Post 8vo. ....*Cloth boards* 1 6

The Story of Creation as told by Theology
AND SCIENCE. By the Rev. T. S. Ackland, M.A. Post 8vo. *Cloth boards* 1 6

Man's Accountableness for his Religious Belief.
A Lecture delivered at the Hall of Science, on Tuesday, April 2nd, 1872. By the Rev. Daniel Moore, M.A., Holy Trinity, Paddington. Post 8vo. ....*Paper cover* 0 3

The Theory of Prayer; with Special Reference
TO MODERN THOUGHT. By the Rev. W. H. Karslake, M.A., Assistant Preacher at Lincoln's Inn, Vicar of Westcott, Dorking. Post 8vo. ....*Limp cloth* 1 0

The Credibility of Mysteries.
A Lecture delivered at St. George's Hall, Langham Place. By the Rev. Daniel Moore, M.A. Post 8vo......*Paper cover* 0 3

Publications on the Christian Evidence.

	Price.
	s. d.

The Gospels of the New Testament: their
GENUINENESS AND AUTHORITY. By the Rev. R. J. Crosthwaite, M.A. Post 8vo.......................*Paper cover* 0 3

Analogy of Religion, Natural and Revealed,
TO THE CONSTITUTION AND COURSE OF NATURE: to which are added, Two Brief Dissertations. By Bishop Butler. NEW EDITION. Post 8vo........................*Cloth boards* 2 6

Christian Evidences:
intended chiefly for the young. By the Most Reverend Richard Whately, D.D. 12mo.................... *Paper cover* 0 4

The Efficacy of Prayer.
By the Rev. W. H. Karslake, M.A., Assistant Preacher at Lincoln's Inn, &c. &c. Post 8vo. .... *Limp cloth* 0 6

Science and the Bible: a Lecture by the Right
Rev. Bishop Perry, D.D. 18mo. *Paper cover* 4d., or *Limp cloth* 0 6

A Lecture on the Bible. By the Very Rev.
E. M. Goulburn, D.D., Dean of Norwich. 18mo. *Paper cover* 0 2

The Bible: Its Evidences, Characteristics, and
EFFECTS. A Lecture by the Right Rev. Bishop Perry, D.D. 18mo..*Paper cover* 0 4

The Origin of the World according to
REVELATION AND SCIENCE. A Lecture by Harvey Goodwin, M.A., Bishop of Carlisle. Post 8vo....*Cloth boards* 0 4

How I passed through Scepticism into Faith.
A Story told in an Almshouse. Post 8vo. ......*Paper cover* 0 3

On the Origin of the Laws of Nature.
By Sir Edmund Beckett, Bart. Post 8vo.......*Cloth boards* 1 6

What is Natural Theology?
Being the Boyle Lectures for 1876. By the Rev. Alfred Barry, D.D., Bishop of Sydney. Post 8vo.......*Cloth boards* 2 6

*** For List of TRACTS on the Christian Evidences, see the Society's Catalogue B.

LONDON:
SOCIETY FOR PROMOTING CHRISTIAN KNOWLEDGE,
NORTHUMBERLAND AVENUE, CHARING CROSS, W.C.;
43, QUEEN VICTORIA STREET, E.C.; 26, 81 GEORGE'S PLACE, S.W.
BRIGHTON; 135, NORTH STREET.

www.ingramcontent.com/pod-product-compliance
Lightning Source LLC
Chambersburg PA
CBHW020310170426
43202CB00008B/563